Antigua and Barbuda: Island Guide

Christopher Beale

Published by
OTHER PLACES PUBLISHING

D0971083

Antigua & Barbuda: Island Guide
Written by: Christopher Beale
Cover designed by: Carla Zetina-Yglesias
Published by:
Other Places Publishing
www.otherplacespublishing.com
www.antiguaislandguide.com

ISBN 978-0-615-21837-3

Printed in the United States of America

Quick Reference

How to Use This Book

The island is organized into 5 sections: St. John's, The Southwest, The Southeast, The East and the North Side. Each section includes directions to sights with an accompanying map. Barbuda also has its own section. Eating, Drinking and Accommodations are organized by these 5 sections and by price.

Exchange Rates

Prices in this book are in Eastern Caribbean Dollars (EC$) or US Dollars (US$). Each are labeled appropriately.
1USD = 2.7EC
1GDP = 5.15EC
1EUR = 4.10EC
1CAD = 2.6EC

Telephone

Country Dialing Code   +268
Emergency   911
See page 46 for emergency and diplomatic contact information

Electricity

Antigua accommodates both 110-120 and 220-240 voltage. Most hotels operate on the American (110-120) system, while the rest of the island uses 220-240. It should be noted that outlets appear to be 110-120 (two flat prongs) but are actually the higher voltage. Always ask before using an outlet.

Business Hours

Banks   Mon-Fri 9:00am-3:00pm;
               Sat 9:00am-noon
Businesses   Mon-Fri 9:00am-6:00pm;
               Sat 9:00am-4:00pm

Quick Stats

Population: 84,000 (2008 est)
Capital (Antigua): St. John's (pop 22,000)
Capital (Barbuda): Codrington (pop 1,000)
Languages: English, local dialect
Land area: 442.6 km^2 (Antigua 280 km^2; Barbuda 161 km^2; Redonda1.6 km^2)
Coastline: 153 km

GDP: 1,526,000,000 (2007 est)
GDP per capita: $18,000 (2007 est)
Unemployment rate: 11% (2001 est)

Number of cruise ship visitors: 470,000 (2006 est)
Number of visitors by air: 250,000 (2007 est)

Type of government: Constitutional monarchy (parliamentary system)
Prime Minister: Baldwin Spencer (United Progressive Party)
Opposition party: Antigua Labour Party

National Symbols...
National bird: Frigate bird (*Fregata magnificens*)
National animal: Fallow deer (*Dama dama)*
National dish: Pepperpot and fungi
National fruit: Antigua black pineapple (*Anana comosus*)
National tree: Widdy widdy bush (*Corchorus siliquosus*)
National flower: Dagger log (*Agave karatto*)

National Holidays...

2008	2009
1 Jan New Year's Day	1 Jan New Year's Day
21 Mar Good Friday	10 Apr Good Friday
24 Mar Easter Monday	13 Apr Easter Monday
5 May Labour Day	4 May Labour Day
12 May Whit Monday	1 Jun Whit Monday
7 Jul Caricom Day	6 Jul Caricom Day
4 August Carnival Monday	3 August Carnival Monday
5 Aug Carnival Tuesday	4 Aug Carnival Tuesday
1 Nov Independence Day	1 Nov Independence Day
9 Dec National Heroes Day	9 Dec National Heroes Day
25-26 Dec Christmas	25-26 Dec Christmas

What's Inside

Maps

ANTIGUA & BARBUDA
Island Guide

Introduction

Antigua (pronounced an-TEE-ga) is a small Caribbean island located in the Leeward Islands of the Lesser Antilles island chain. The 108 square mile island is complimented by Barbuda lying just 27 miles to the north and the uninhabited Redonda, 24 miles to the southwest. Approximately 70,000 people live on Antigua, all residing in the capital of St. John's or in the numerous villages sprawled across the island.

Antigua's international reputation is rooted in the beaches that stretch seemingly endlessly across its shores. The soft white sand and crystal clear water with shades of blue found only here attract thousands of visitors every year. There is no doubt that Antigua and Barbuda have some of the nicest beaches in the Caribbean, if not the world. Although these beaches should not be missed, there is much to see and experience along the way.

Antigua is rumored to have 365 beaches – one for every day of the year.

With a burgeoning tourism mindset, Antigua is quickly becoming a major player in the Caribbean tourist industry. St. John's cruise ship docks can handle over 15,000 visitors a day and

V.C. Bird Int'l Airport has recently been renovated to accommodate the influx of tourists to the island. Foreign investment is quickly developing otherwise unspoiled beachfront property and local tour operators have followed suit creating well organized tour packages to fit any personality.

Parts of Antigua still remain untouched by developers and most of the local population hopes to keep it that way. Although tourism is considered necessary for the island's economic development, Antiguans are aware of the importance of preserving their national identity and culture. A culture they are happy to share with those wishing to experience the Antiguan way of life.

ONE DAY IN ANTIGUA

The morning starts early. I stop at a roadside vendor to buy a salt fish sandwich topped with avocado, tomato, lettuce and, of course, Susie's Hot Sauce. Sorrell is in season so I buy a glass and continue towards English Harbour. Passing school children in neatly pressed uniforms, several goats meander across the road forcing me to yield. The cool morning air is fading into a sunny, hot day.

I eat my breakfast while roaming through Nelson's Dockyard (pg 75), absorbing the historical atmosphere and reading about the history of the area at the Dockyard Museum (pg 75). I take the short walk to Fort Berkeley (pg 76), and then head over to Falmouth Harbour (pg 74) to see the magnificent ships in port. The restaurants are now opening for lunch and although a roti from Grace Before Meals (pg 112) sounds appealing, I decide to leave the area for more exploring.

I turn left out of English Harbour towards Liberta (pg 72) where I stop to grab a *ting* before passing through Tyrells, admiring the grandeur of

Our Lady of Perpetual Help (pg 72) along the way. Turning left down Fig Tree Drive, I soon become engulfed in a verdant forest speckled with mango and banana trees. Turning off at Wallings Nature Reserve (pg 69), I take a small hike exploring the forest around the Victorian era structures.

As I leave Wallings, I stop to enjoy a freshly sliced black pineapple (pg 68) from the Culture Shop located just at the nature reserve's entrance. Popping the slices into my mouth, I drive towards Old Road (pg 68) passing the rows of neatly planted pineapple at Claremont Farms (pg 68).

With the sun high in the sky and the heat inescapable, the calm Caribbean Sea at Morris Bay is beckoning. I jump out of the car for a quick swim. The water is contagious so I head up to one of my favorites, Dark Wood Beach (pg 59).

The sun begins to dip in the horizon and Montserrat (pg 64) becomes ever so clear. Guadeloupe can be seen in the distance behind the volcanic island, with Redonda (pg 65) and Nevis to the right.

On my way back north along the coastline, I stop at Ffryes Beach to use the outdoor freshwater showers before having a lobster dinner at Sheer Restaurant (pg 110). The sun is now just setting and the views over the Caribbean Sea are unimaginable.

After a full day of exploring the Dockyard, taking in Fig Tree Drive, and doing a bit of beach hopping, I'm ready to *lime* in St. John's. The first stop is at Funky Buddha (pg 117) where I enjoy a couple *Wadadlis* on the small deck overlooking Redcliffe Street. Now that the dinner crowd has left, I hire a taxi to take me north to Dickenson Bay. The Beach Restaurant (pg 120) has turned into an open air nightclub right on the water. The island's elite are in the back dancing, drinking at the bar, or seeking privacy on the beach. Loosened up, I head back to St. John's and down to the Dominican district where the late-night bars are filling up. Merengue music blasts from embedded speakers in the walls as I order a *Presidente* to settle in for a long night.

TOP 10 SIGHTS AND ACTIVITIES

Walking tour of St. John's (pg 52)

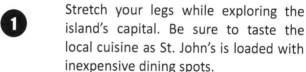

Stretch your legs while exploring the island's capital. Be sure to taste the local cuisine as St. John's is loaded with inexpensive dining spots.

Explore Betty's Hope (pg 83)

Once the largest sugar plantation on Antigua, Betty's Hope features the only restored sugar mill on the island and the estate is a reminder of an earlier time.

Snorkeling at Great Bird Island (pg 84)

Many tour operators offer full day packages to this uninhabited isle. It's not hard to see why with two deserted beaches and a reef system that supports an abundance of marine life.

Day-trip to Barbuda (pg 130)

Spend a day on one of the few untouched islands left in the Caribbean. Beach comb miles of pink sand, explore shipwrecks off Barbuda's shores, or stroll through the lazy streets of Codrington.

Enjoy an ocean cruise (pg 98)

Whether it's a private yacht charter, catamaran tour or eco-adventure, be sure to get out on the water and have some fun!

Admire the southwest coast sunset

You may see the infamous green flash but if not don't worry, you'll forget all about it when the sun dips into the Caribbean Sea and the sky fills with radiant bursts of color. The views of smoldering Montserrat are a nice touch, too.

Barbeque at Shirley Heights (pg 78)

The island's biggest party spot is filled with locals and tourists eating, drinking and dancing to live music well into the evening.

Lime at Half Moon Bay (pg 88)

Arguably the finest beach on Antigua, Half Moon is a pristine specimen of what a Caribbean beach should be. Don't forget to stop by Smiling Harry's (pg 120) for a burger and a story or two.

Visit Nelson's Dockyard (pg 75)

Once the Royal Navy's strongest fortification in the Eastern Caribbean, this naval yard has been beautifully restored and allows the visitor to step back in time to Antigua's colonial era.

Cruise through Fig Tree Drive (pg 68)

The island's only existing tropical forest, Fig Tree Drive takes the traveler through fields of banana, mango, breadfruit and other tropical vegetation.

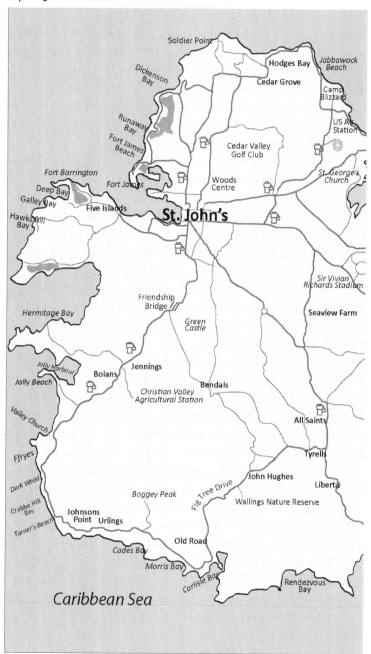

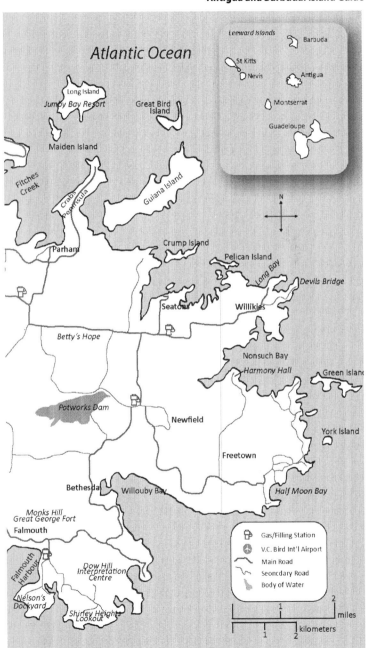

History

FIRST INHABITANTS

The earliest settlements on Antigua date back to 2900BC to a people known as the Ciboney, a pre-agricultural Amerindian tribe from South America. These seafaring wanderers were mostly hunters and gathers living off Antigua's abundant flora and fauna. Evidence of their existence on Antigua is limited but sites, like those found at Jolly Beach and around Parham, have been discovered dating to these first inhabitants.

Originating from Venezuela, the Arawaks arrived around 35AD. Bringing more advanced agricultural techniques and tools to the island, the Arawaks lived peacefully for over a thousand years. Their settlements and artifacts have been discovered at over 40 sites across Antigua and Barbuda, including at Indian Town (pg 87), Mamora Bay and Spanish Point (pg 135) in Barbuda. In addition, megaliths at Green Castle Hill (pg 62) are thought to be part of an astronomical observatory and temple linked to the Arawaks.

The nonviolent Arawaks easily succumbed to the bellicose Carib tribe that waged a war path across the Caribbean around 1100AD. With their superior seafaring ability (boats were known to have as many as 100 oars and have the capability to seize European ships) and advanced weapons, the Caribs easily conquered the Arawaks enslaving and killing many. The Arawaks were eventually forced to flee Antigua with many settling on the northern islands of Jamaica and Puerto Rico.

The only Carib population in the Caribbean Islands today is on a protected reservation in Dominica where 3,000 Caribs live.

The Caribs, however, did not create settlements on Antigua. Rather, they used the island as a provisioning station and as a base for attacks on other islands. The Carib's military might would later test even the strongest European powers during the early stages of colonization.

EUROPEAN CONTACT

When Christopher Columbus sailed past a tiny island in the Caribbean, he looked out and proclaimed it Santa Maria de la Antigua after the church in Seville – he never stepped foot on the island. Antigua continued to be ignored by European powers for nearly 150 more years until a group of Englishmen from St. Kitts ventured to Antigua in 1632 and proclaimed it in the name of the Queen. This small group of men, led by a young Captain Edward Warner who had established the first colony on St. Kitts, settled in the area around Falmouth. Newly arrived, these settlers organized small crop production and lived off the land but would continually be harassed by the Caribs. Despite often bloody raids from the interloping tribe, Warner and his men persevered. The European settlement of Antigua had begun.

Wadadli

Wadadli, the Carib name given to the island, has been adopted by numerous local businesses from the island's unofficial beer to tour operators. The Caribs gave the name Wa'omoni to Barbuda and the Caribbean Sea takes its name from the Caribs.

KING SUGAR AND SLAVERY

In 1674, after a brief occupation of Antigua by French forces, a wealthy plantation owner from Barbados named Sir Christopher Codrington was granted the rights to Betty's Hope sugar plantation by the Crown of England. At the time, tobacco was the main cash crop on Antigua but due to a saturated market, the value of the plant was quickly falling. Codrington entered the sugar era at

CANNIBALISM IN THE CARIBBEAN?

The Caribs are rumored to have incorporated cannibalism into their religious ceremonies (although some contemporary historians dispute this claim). In fact, the English word "cannibal" originated from the Carib word for person, karibna. The Hollywood blockbuster Pirates of the Caribbean didn't help this stereotype with the film's star, Johnny Depp, being prepared as a ceremonial feast by an indigenous Caribbean tribe.

a time when the popularity of sugar throughout Europe was growing. He quickly developed the sugar production capacity of Antigua and implemented advanced methods of refining sugar at Betty's Hope (he would later lease the island of Barbuda for provisioning purposes, see page 132 for a brief history of Barbuda). Codrington would eventually become the largest landowner and richest planter in the Leeward Islands.

Word of Codrington's success quickly spread across the plantocracy of the West Indies and by 1748 nearly 175 sugar mills were operating on the island. The verdant land that covered the island was cleared to maximize the land area for sugar cane, which soon replaced the tropical forests. Antigua transformed into a major asset in the era of King Sugar and, during its peak, created more wealth than the entire North American continent.

Nearly 100 sugar mills remain on the island.

Unlike tobacco, which relied upon a small pool of indentured servants, sugar plantations required a large labor force to sustain the intensive production efforts. Britain, therefore, imported as many as 12 million men, women and children in the bonds of slavery across their empire. By the

FORTIFICATION OF THE ISLAND

Realizing the strategic importance of Antigua, Britain built over 40 military installations across the island during its rule. Such fortifications protected the valuable sugar industry from prying European powers and deterred any looming Caribs. The most famous of these installments is located at English Harbour, where Nelson's Dockyard (pg 75) has been restored to a remarkable condition and is the only working Georgian naval dockyard in the world today.

In addition to Nelson's Dockyard, there are several forts to explore on Antigua and Barbuda. Some have been restored, but many are simply ruins.

Fort James (pg 91)	Shirley Heights (pg 77)
Fort Barrington (pg 61)	Fort Berkeley (pg 76)
Great George Fort (pg 74)	Martello Tower, Barbuda (pg 135)

mid 1700s, slaves outnumbered whites 10 to 1 with the number of Africans enslaved on Antigua peaking at 37,500 in 1770.

In 1736 a group of slaves plotted an uprising to overthrow the white establishment. The plan called for three parties of 350 slaves to converge on St. John's and kill the colonists who were to gather at a party honoring the coronation of George II. The party, however, was delayed until the King's birthday and the plot was eventually uncovered. Three ring leaders were identified and "broken at the wheel" while another sixty slaves were brutally killed.

EMANCIPATION

Emancipation came in 1834 when Britain abolished slavery across its empire. For the 23,500 newly freed Antiguans life on the island changed very little. They continued to work on the plantations, but for very low wages now. Black Antiguans lived in wattle houses made from sticks and mud while the plantocracy actually benefited from paying the freed laborers directly since it was cheaper than maintaining the slave system. For the next 100 years as sugar production weaned and prices for the once valuable commodity fell, life for black Antiguans worsened even further to a state of near destitution.

LABOR MOVEMENT AND INDEPENDENCE

In 1939 a Royal Commission was ordered to investigate the deteriorating living conditions on Antigua. Upon arriving on the island, the Moyne Commission, named after its chairman, found abominable living and working conditions. In response to the commission's report, the Antigua Trades and Labour Union (ATLU) was created empowering laborers with unprecedented leverage in negotiating better pay rates and securing labor rights. In 1943 a young Vere Cornwall Bird became its president leading the struggle against exploitive and unfair labor practices.

In 1951 adult suffrage was proclaimed and the Antigua Labour Party (ALP), under the ATLU, won all legislative seats. The ALP would continue to control these seats until 1967, effectively solidifying its place in the Antiguan political arena. Throughout this period, V.C. Bird's political strength grew and through numerous concessions by the British, he was appointed Chief Minister in 1960. In 1967 Antigua was appointed Associated State of the Commonwealth giving the small island control of its internal affairs. Fourteen years later, in 1981, Antigua and Barbuda gained its independence from Britain and V.C. Bird was named Antigua and Barbuda's first Prime Minister.

THE BIRD DYNASTY

As a champion and leader of the people during British rule, V.C. Bird symbolized Antiguan freedom. The young charismatic leader rode into power on a wave of support that seemed imperturbable. "Papa Bird" as he was affectionately called, navigated the country away from sugar production – he associated this and other agricultural trades to remnants of the slave era – and set Antigua's course towards tourism. Hotels sprouted around the island with foreign investment pouring in. The economy grew commensurate with V.C. Bird's political strength resulting in a crash course for corruption and scandal.

Today, tourism accounts for 70% of Antigua's economy.

V.C. Bird received his first taste of scandal in 1977 when he allowed Space Research, a Canadian-American weapons company owned by Gerald Bull, to operate in Antigua. The agreement stated that the company would not be held to custom procedures, thus allowing importation and exportation of goods without any trace of the materials (in this case, military weapons). The agreement also allowed international buyers discreet travel to Antigua without documentation. It wasn't until a crane crashed carrying a container full of 155mm howitzers being loaded for export that the operation was exposed. A local opposition newspaper quickly latched on to the story and international media outlets followed suit. It was soon discovered that the company had been shipping arms to the white minority government of South Africa. Gerald Bull and Space Research quietly withdrew from the country. Bull would later be found shot to death in Belgium where he was reportedly working on a "super gun" for Saddam Hussein.

Vere Bird Jr., V.C.'s son, gained international notoriety in 1990 when a cache of assault weapons that were purchased by the government of Antigua were discovered with the Gacha drug cartel in Colombia. The weapons were part of a legal shipment from Israel for the Antigua and Barbuda Defense Force but was furtively diverted to Colombia. Vere Bird Jr., now a powerful politician and member of Cabinet, signed for the shipment before it vanished from the island. The international scandal brought condemnation for the tiny Caribbean island and Bird Junior was forced to resign from his Cabinet post. No charges, however, were brought against him.

The scandals continued throughout the 1990s and became more blatant as in the case of Ivor Bird, the youngest of the Bird sons, who was caught with 25 pounds of cocaine while trying to board a plane out of Antigua. He was quietly fined for the attempted drug smuggling.

In Jamaica Kincaid's internationally acclaimed memoir, *A Small Place*, she writes with contempt of the corruption of the government and the passivity of the Antiguan people during this time. While the average Antiguan lived in poverty, she states, the ruling elite enjoyed the luxuries of the British who preceded them. The Antiguan people simply replaced one form of ruling elite for another. Kincaid describes this period in Antiguan history as "a monument to rottenness".

V.C. Bird eventually handed the reigns of power to his son Lester Bird who became Prime Minister in 1994 and won reelection in 1999. Soon after, in June 1999, Papa Bird passed away and with him the political stronghold he kept over the country.

POLITICS TODAY

In 2004 the ALP saw its power officially weakened as the United Progressive Party (UPP), formed in 1992 as a coalition of opposition political parties, won 55% of the popular vote and 12 of the 17 seats in Parliament. Voted in on a platform of reform and a promise to restore the integrity of the country, the UPP ousted the Bird dynasty from power for the first time in 23 years.

Political Colors

On government buildings and public domains, the blue and yellow colors of the UPP have literally replaced the red and white of the ALP.

People You Should Know
BALDWIN SPENCER

Leader of the United Progressive Party and current Prime Minister of the twin island nation, Baldwin Spencer is seen by many to be a straightforward and honest man. He keeps a low profile and can often be sighted at community events and gatherings with just one personal body guard. If you happen to spot him, his congenial and charismatic nature offers visitors the chance to chat with a national leader.

Since taking control, the UPP has struggled to fulfill its platform of improved roads, construction of community centers, and government wage increases.

The new government has consistently placed blame for these shortcomings on the previous administration and a disdainful atmosphere has developed between ALP and UPP political supporters. Antiguans will talk long and hard about who is best fit to lead. On the streets of St. John's it is common to hear, "me'a ALP man, dis new govment mash up every'ting!"

Culture

NATIONAL IDENTITY

"100% Antiguan me'a be" is a proud statement in Antigua, one that Antiguans will assert anytime their lineage is questioned. Although they are definitely part of a larger West Indian population from Jamaica to Trinidad, Antiguans see themselves as a cut above the rest. This may be simply nationalistic pride, a healthy dose in fact, but such an attitude can sometimes come across as rude and pompous to the visitor. Antiguans can be cool. A little too cool, in fact.

Much of this stems from the increase of immigrants from other Caribbean islands, especially the Dominican Republic. Antigua today is a mix of cultures from across the region and unfortunately xenophobia has taken root in some circles of the country. Dominicans are often held responsible for the illegal brothels that are allowed to run freely on the island, and Jamaicans are endlessly blamed for the increasing crime rate.

There is also a relatively large population of Middle Eastern businessmen (and their families) who have established successful businesses and restaurants. You may notice young middle eastern

LIMING

Liming is relaxing under a tamarind tree while drinking the jelly from a freshly plucked coconut; strolling down the streets of St. John's on a late Friday afternoon; or just sitting on the street corner playing a round of dominoes with friends. Liming is the favorite pastime of Antigua – it's the art of just cooling-out.

men carrying large duffels bags through the villages; they are door-to-door salesmen representing businesses in St. John's.

RELIGION AND PROPRIETY

Religions Represented
(2001 est)
Anglican 25.7%
Seventh Day Adventist 12.3%
Pentecostal 10.6%
Moravian 10.5%
Roman Catholic 10.4%
Methodist 7.9%
Baptist 4.9%
Church of God 4.5%
Other Christian 5.4%
Other 2%
None or unspecified

Religion, specifically Christianity, plays a major role in Antiguan life. Almost every denomination is present and the island shuts down on Sunday as churches fill-up across the nation. Prayers are encouraged in public schools, official meetings, and any other opportunity that may arise. It is important for the visitor to remember that Antiguans frown upon public drunkenness, beachwear (other than on the beach, of course), and even smoking in public.

An interesting contrast to Antigua's cool and laidback atmosphere is a well entrenched (and practiced) culture of manners. The most evident is when meeting someone to say "Good Morning", "Good Afternoon" or "Good Evening/Night". It is considered rude by many Antiguans to initiate a conversation without first greeting the other in this fashion. When entering a shop, always greet the attendant first and you will be surprised at the difference in the reaction you receive – from being ignored to near alacrity.

SPORTS

Antigua is filled with Sport. Youth are especially gifted at a number of athletics but cricket and football (or soccer, as the British term is used on the island) dominate the athletic scene. Every village is equipped with a "playing field" that is used for both football and cricket. Football season runs April through January with village leagues preceding the Premier, or professional, league. There is a poorly funded and ill-equipped national team that competes regionally with mixed results.

Cricket is a remnant of the British ruling elite but Antigua has adopted it as its own. The official season runs from January to July where local leagues compete against one another and the beloved West Indies Cricket team battles for international domination. If you aren't in the mood to sit through a five day match, the Stanford 20/20 Cricket Tournament, held January through February, offers a fast pace, intense competition that draws national teams from across the Caribbean. The games are held at the cricket grounds by the airport and it's a great place to see the sport enjoyed by locals and visitors.

Find More... **ON THE WEB**

www.windiescricket.com
www.stanford2020.com

Although not really an athletic sport, warri and dominoes are enjoyed by an older generation of Antiguans. You will notice men sitting around tables in the villages playing dominoes for hours at a time with crowds gathering now and again to see the game played at its best. A single game of dominoes may only last for a small amount of time, but is played throughout the day in a tournament style of play. Warri, a game originating in Africa, is played by capturing an opponent's marbles (or, traditionally, warri seeds) by strategically aligning

People You Should Know
SIR VIVIAN RICHARDS

Sir Vivian Richards is quite arguably Antigua's national hero since he embodies the sport for which Antiguans go crazy over: cricket. Three time captain of the West Indies cricket team, Sir Viv captured the heart of Antigua when he scored the fastest test century against England at the Antigua Recreation Grounds in 1986. The bat "Master Blaster" used is on display at the Museum of Antigua and Barbuda in St. John's.

your own throughout a wooden board.

THE MEDIA

The media plays a major role in Antigua. Every morning partisan radio talk show hosts verbally bash their opponents with long diatribes to emote listeners. The *Daily Observer* newspaper could be likened to a gossip column with the latest scandals floating around the island. The *Antigua Sun* is a more reputable news source but much less entertaining. Each can be purchased at a variety of locations.

Find More...
ON THE WEB
www.antiguasun.com
www.antiguaobserver.com

The Antigua and Baruba Broadcasting Service (ABS) is the only local television channel and provides local news nightly along with coverage of local events. *Good Morning Antigua and Barbuda*, a local morning show, provides an outlet for pundits, artists and information on the general happenings around the island.

THE LANGUAGE – DIALECT

Chups

Chups is a sound made by sucking the front teeth to express displeasure or dissatisfaction. A common form of expression on Antigua.

English is the official language of Antigua and Barbuda but an island dialect is often used. It is a mixture of Antiguan and British slang, broken English, and African terms fragmented and spoken very quickly. There is no official dictionary to reference or set rules to follow, but if you want to learn more about the language you can check out local author Joy Lawrence's book *The Way We Talk* (available at Best of Books in St. Johns, see pg 58).

LEARN DIALECT

A way you go? Where are you going?	*Dis sweet me bad.* It's funny/nice.
Me a go beach. I'm going to the beach.	*Me nah nyam.* I'm not eating.
Town me a go. I'm going to St. John's	*A wa ta joke?* Are you seroius?
Fu ture? Really?	*Me garn.* I'm leaving
Jus cross dey. Just over there.	*Eveyrting mash up.* Broken, ruined.
Me long fu see you. I miss(ed) you.	*Tall!* No way, not at all.
Walk with... Bring it with you.	*Me nah know.* I don't know.

Ms. Lawrence has researched the history of the language and has created a working dictionary.

LITERATURE

Reading the works of local authors is a great way to gain insight into the culture of the island, and Antigua has plenty:

Jamaica Kincaid: Her 1988 work A Small Place won international acclaim and has been causing controversy ever since. The memoir places the blame for Antigua's corruption squarely on Britain's quest for domination and despises the passivity of the Antiguan public. She goes on to deride the tourists and shows a rare side of the average Antiguan.

Buying books in Antigua
You can purchase these books along with other works by local authors at *Best of Books* (pg 58) in St. John's . Many are also available at online retailers.

Joanne C. Hillhouse: A local writer and journalist, Hillhouse has authored two books of which *Dancing Nude in the Moonlight* is her most recognized. Hillhouse's work gives a descriptive and poignant look at the Antiguan culture.

Joy Lawrence: Joy Lawrence has been documenting Antiguan culture her entire life. Her works include poetry, short stories, non-fiction and documenting the local dialect. She is best known for writing in dialect.

Keithlyn B. Smith and Fernando C. Smith: These two brothers cowrote *To Shoot Hard Labor*. The book offers insight into the poorer classes on the island during slavery and emancipation thereafter.

Robert Coram: An American journalist based in Antigua during the Bird reign, Coram wrote an exposé of the corruption that ran rampant on the island. *Caribbean Time Bomb* was first published in 1993 and immediately banned in Antigua. Coram has not returned since (the Bird's apparently made it clear he was not welcomed) but the book has and can now be purchased on the island.

Desmond Nicholson: Desmond Nicholson has authored numerous books recording the history of Antigua and Barbuda. His entire collection, covering everything from the Arawaks to Antigua's landmarks, can be found at the National Museum.

MUSIC

Soca and reggae dominate the airwaves of local radio stations. Local artisits like Tizzy, Claudette Peters, El A Kru and the Burning Flames are favorites. Regional artists such as Beenie Man, Destra Garcia and Elephant Man get serious attention, too. The classic reggae of Bob Marley is alive and well with his timeless *Legends* album being the unofficial soundtrack of the Caribbean.

Calypso is considered a specialty on Antigua and it can be heard across the island on radio, television and live at nearly every public event. Originating in West Africa, slaves sang calypso as an artisitic outlet for their daily struggle in the bonds of slavery. Calypsonians today carry on that tradition by referencing social and economic discontenct while often taking shots at prominent public figures, especially elected officials.

Steel pan is much revered amongst the population. It truly is considered Antigua's export to the world and they absolutely have something to boast about. If you have the chance, be sure to

Find More...
ON THE WEB
Antigua will host its first annual Romantic Rymths Music Festival in June 2008 featuring international musical acts and local artists.
www.antiguamusicfestival.com

Music You Should Know
BURNING FLAMES

Four brothers created this local band in 1986 and the Flames have dominated the Antiguan music scene since, especially during Carnival. The death of the lead singer Onika Bostic in 2004 drove the core members to create their own projects such as the Red Hot Flames and 3-Cylinder, each playing regularly on the island. But the Burning Flames still regroup and play together to the delight of their strong local following.

hear a live steel band orchestra like the *Gemonites* perform or, better yet, *Panorama* (the island's biggest steel pan orchestra competition) during Carnival (pg 30).

Americanization

As with so many other societies around the world, Antigua has succumbed to the attractive culture of the United States. Hip-hop music and Black Entertainment Television (BET) are controversial subjects for the older generation of Antiguans as they are witnessing their youth gravitate towards a more violent and vulgar form of exprssion. Hip-hop is popular with many youth and can be found on ipods across the island. Some Antiguans are publicly attributing the swelling of youth violence to this imported culture.

SAILING WEEK

With strong winds and smooth Caribbean waters, Antigua is a sailing paradise. Every year the small island is inundated with over 5,000 sailors and 250 vessels from around the world. The last week of April and beginning of May is intended to be a racing competition around the island amongst various classes. With so many visitors, partying and hedonism are sure to follow and each night festivities take hold, typically centered around English Harbour with one night dedicated to Jolly Harbour. There are also beach bashes, like on lay day, held at Pigeon Beach (pg 76) and Dickenson Bay (pg 92).

Find More...
ON THE WEB
www.sailingweek.com
www.antiguaclassics.com

The week prior to Sailing Week is known as Classic Sailing Week and it is a time for more traditional vessels to take to the seas in a competitive week. About 50-60 ships that cannot competitively compete against more modern sail boats, set sail in a similar yet somehow classier race.

CARNIVAL

Barbuda's Carnival, *Caribana,* is held every June

Every year for ten days leading up to the first Tuesday in August, Antigua transforms: Government workers ditch their stuffy suits for colorful and skimpy outfits, drink rum and dance down the streets of St. John's; villages begin practicing steel pan late into the evening in hopes their steel orchestra will win *Panorama*; and tourists come to the island to see Antigua come alive with celebration. Carnival is a time of dancing, music and festivities with everyone on the island participating.

The first unofficial Carnival took place on August 1 1834 after Britain abolished slavery across its empire. Liberated slaves took to the streets in celebration of their new freedom. Each year thereafter the first Monday in August was set aside as a holiday to commemorate emancipation. In 1957 the holiday was extended to include the following Tuesday to allow longer, more organized celebrations including a parade and beauty pageant.

Since then Carnival has developed into a ten day celebration that takes over the island. Most of the activities are centered in St. John's as the

People You Should Know
ALLEN STANFORD

Allen Stanford is a controversial figure and Antiguans either love him or hate him. An American billionaire from Houston, Stanford first set his eyes on Antigua in the 1980s and has since developed a regional airline, the Antigua Sun newspaper, several resorts and a financial group (amongst other ventures). Many would claim he is slowly buying up the island and holds more power than its elected officials. Others argue he greatly contributes to development and his philanthropic causes offer assistance to the local people. Whichever is the case, his mark is immediately felt by the arriving visitor with the superbly well landscaped area around V.C. Bird Int'l Airport including the Sticky Wicket Restaurant (pg 115) and adjoining cricket stadium where his annual Stanford 20/20 Cricket Tournament is held.

Antigua Recreation Grounds (ARG) is transformed into *Carnival City* with nightly shows such as *Panorama, Soca Monarch* and *Carnival Queen*. The biggest attractions are the *Calypso King* and *Queen* competitions that spark up well before the shows with performers hitting the local media outlets taunting their rivals and promoting themselves.

The well organized events of Carnival City attract almost all of the island's residents and a *shantytown*, as it is known, is erected around the ARG. Locals sell barbeque and cold drinks out of makeshift stalls, and liming (with gambling and other mischievous acts) continue until dawn. The best known shantytown is inside the East Bus Station with construction of temporary shelters beginning well in advance of the celebrations.

All celebrations lead to *J'ouvert*, a must for any visitor interested in all-night partying through St. John's. The festivities begin Monday night and last through the evening until 4am when J'ouvert morning begins. A huge parade with everyone participating roars down the streets of St. John's. Dancing, loud music and drinking merge for a moving party that lasts well into the morning. Troupes follow their floats – which are usually just trucks filled with loud speakers and drinks – while jumping around the streets like no one is watching.

Tuesday, the last day of Carnival, hosts the final parade in the afternoon with a culminating ceremony at Carnival City. This is really the sane version of the J'ouvert celebration with the traditional colorful costumes and well designed floats. Then planning and anticipation begin for the next year.

Find More...
ON THE WEB
www.antiguacarnival.com

Environment

Cassie Bush is a term used to describe the low-lying, prickly bush that covers the island.

Even those who espouse the corruption of government officials or balk at the impervious rude attendant will admit that the beauty of Antigua is undeniable, and it's everywhere. The crystal clear waters with the amazing shades of blue they project are accented by rolling hills. Spectacular vistas are offered on almost every hilltop, and the beaches are second to none.

GEOGRAPHY & TOPOGRAPHY

Located in the Leeward Island chain, Antigua is relatively flat and dry compared to some of the other Eastern Caribbean islands to the south. This unique topography gives the island its long stretches of white sand beach but also limits the rainfall the island receives resulting in no rivers or streams.

The Shekerly Mountain range stretches along the southwest coast with Boggy Peak (pg 67) being the highest point on the island at 1,319 ft (402 m). This area is also the most fertile as a trip down Fig Tree Drive (pg 68) displays banana plantations, mango trees and pineapple farms.

THE ANTIGUAN RACER & THE MONGOOSE

Antigua is home to many species of animals, but its most famous resident was introduced to eradicate the rat infestation European settlers brought with them. The Asian mongoose had one purpose: to kill the black rats that snuck onto the island aboard slave ships. The small predator, however, began to devour other species including the Antiguan Racer snake. Rats were not eradicated and the mongoose population thrived (you will notice them scurrying alongside the road today), but within sixty years the Antiguan Racer snake became extinct. Or so experts thought. In

Find More...
ON THE WEB
www.eag.org.ag
www.antiguanracer.org

the early 1990s the snake was discovered on the mongoose-free isle of Great Bird Island (pg 84), off the shores of Antigua. Since then, the Environmental Awareness Group and the Antiguan Racer Conservation Project have worked to protect what is thought to be the rarest snake in the world.

AN IMPORTED ENVIRONMENT

At one time Antigua was a verdant, tropical island. Then came King Sugar and with it the destruction of the island's natural environment to clear land for the production of the valuable commodity. To compensate for the destruction and to introduce edible vegetation, the British imported various plants from their colonies around the world: papaya and mango trees from India; breadfruit from Tahiti; even the postcard print coconut palm, which has become the revered symbol of Caribbean tranquility, is not indigenous to the island.

THE BASICS

Getting There

If you are traveling from the U.S., several airlines offer service to Antigua: American, Delta, U.S. Airways and Continental. In addition, Air Canada offers service along with Caribbean Airlines, which has non-stop flights from New York and Miami. From the UK, Virgin and British Airways offer regular non-stop service to the island.

Flexible Days = Cheaper Fares

If you are flexible with travel dates, try orbitz.com's flexible search to find the lowest fares from various airlines over a combination of dates. The more flexible you are with your dates, the better chance you have of getting the lowest fare.

Antigua makes a great starting point for exploring the islands, as the regional carrier Liat has its hub in Antigua. One-way fares can start as low as US$35 for travel to St. Kitts, or up to US$150 for travel to Guyana. Caribbean Airlines also offers service from Antigua to select

Caribbean countries including Trinidad, Grenada, Barbados and Suriname.

Liat Airlines
1-888-844-5428 or 480-5601
www.liatairline.com

Caribbean Airlines
1-800-538-2942 or 480-2900
www.caribbeanairlines.com

Getting Around

Due to its small size and flat surface, Antigua is easy and fast to get around. Examining any map, you may be confused by the lack of street names; that's because there are none (except in St. John's). "Main roads" run from St. John's outward to villages and coastal areas. The villages have smaller unnamed roads leading from the main road, connecting communities. Landmarks are used in place of street names and numbers. It is common to ask directions and receive, in response, "take the main road to the church and take a left at the shop".

As a former British colony, all cars drive on the left.

But as a visitor the island's small size and simplicity make it easy to navigate (and fun to explore!). Don't be afraid to stop at a local shop to ask for directions while sipping a *ting* (grapefruit soda) and chatting with the locals.

V.C. BIRD INT'L AIRPORT

First impressions are always important, yet Antigua has continued to struggle to impress arriving visitors. Stepping onto the tarmac, you immediately absorb the warm Caribbean air with the soothing cool trade winds. A steel pan musician is playing welcoming melodies as you enter the terminal and you think, *this is it, I am in paradise*. Then reality sets in. Long lines, surly immigration agents, and disdainful customs officers are the unofficial welcome agents to the island. The baggage claim is more of a free-for-all with porters running about and unattended luggage everywhere. V.C. Bird Int'l Airport is a problem for Antigua and one that officials have recognized. For the 2007 Cricket World Cup, the airport underwent renovations that were meant to increase the capacity of the airport to handle the rise in visitors the island is

CAR RENTAL

Car rentals are the main mode of transportation for most visitors. Antigua has numerous rental agencies from familiar names like Hertz and Avis to locally owned and operated companies, each accommodating airport pick-up and drop-off. All vehicle types are available but if you are planning on exploring some of the island's more remote areas, a four-wheel drive might be a good option.

A temporary license is required costing EC$50/US$20 and can be obtained at the rental company. Be sure to have your national or international license with you. Depending on the season, the cost of a car is usually around US$40-$60 a day.

Car Rental Agencies

Avis	**Tropical Rentals**
462-2840	562-5181
www.avis.com	www.tropicalrentalsantigua.com
Hertz	**Titi Rent-A-Car**
481-4440	460-1452
www.hertz.com	Email: titi@candw.ag

Driving Conditions

Renting a car gives you the freedom and flexibility to explore the island, but driving on Antigua can be a challenge. Antiguans complain about the poor conditions of the roads with potholes slowing traffic on both main and local roads. Stray animals, like goats and cattle, often wander onto the streets and have been known to cause confusion if not accidents. Not to mention the lack of traffic law enforcement (what traffic laws?); beware of speeding cars that will pass you even if there is oncoming traffic! Antiguans have figured out how to squeeze three cars onto the two-lane main roads.

TAXI SERVICE

Taxis are in abundance, but unfortunately supply and demand economics do not dictate the price. The government sets all prices with little room for negotiation with your driver.

There are several taxi stands in St. John's and most resort areas have taxis readily available. But it is always good to carry a few telephone numbers for reliable taxi service providers.

Antigua 24hr Taxi
460-5353

Heritage Quay Taxi
460-8213

United Taxi Assoc.
562-0262

BUS SYSTEM

The bus system on Antigua is convenient and reliable with two main terminals in St. John's: the East Bus Station catering to the east side of the island, and the more organized West Bus Station running buses to the south and west side.

All buses are privately owned with a union dictating the prices, which vary from EC$2.00-$3.75 depending on the distance of travel. Almost all the drivers take U.S. currency and charge about US$1-2 each way. Bus drivers rarely accept bills larger than EC$20, and can only make change in Eastern Caribbean dollars.

The procedure for the buses is pretty simple: each lines up in there designated spot at one of the two bus terminals and loads passengers one at a time. Unlike most Caribbean countries, Antigua's buses do not carry more than the standard fourteen passengers per van (more for larger buses). Jump seats in the isle are used to maximize space and there is plenty of room to be comfortable. When one bus is full, it leaves and another bus takes its place. There are no set time schedules, but buses can depart as quickly as every five minutes to as long as thirty minutes. The #20 (to Jolly Harbour) and #17 (to English Harbour) are the most frequent with departures every five to ten minutes.

Running Hours
If you are returning late, ask the driver what time the last bus runs. Most buses will stop operating after 7:00pm. The #22 and #17 buses, however, operate late into the evening.

To get a bus *to* St. John's, just stand by the side of the main road until a van passes with "BUS" on the license plate (buses only run on main roads). Flag the driver and board. Wait until you arrive at your destination before paying.

The Name Game

Most drivers give their buses unique and creative names to distinguish themselves from others. Keep in Touch, Jah Ride, Cool Ruler, and the deviant No Name are just a few. Drivers have recently outfitted their vehicles with DVD players and state-of-the-art sound systems giving the passenger a ride to remember.

MOPED AND BICYCLE RENTAL

Other options for getting around include moped and bicycle rentals. Serious safety issues should be considered before choosing these alternatives. First, as previously mentioned, traffic can be very hazardous especially for the leisure bicyclist. Although the government has tried to crack down on speeding, some drivers insist on recklessly racing down curvy main roads. There are no bike lanes.

The heat is another concern. The tropics offer a more intense heat that can be deceivingly exhausting. Plenty of water should be carried along with adequate protection from the sun.

Bike Plus Limited
St. John's; 462-2453
www.bikeplusantigua.com
Rents an assortment of mountain bikes for all sizes; US$17/day per bike.

Cheke's Scooter Rental
Falmouth; 562-4646
chekesscooter@hotmail.com
Scooter rentals for around
US$40/day; US$225/week.

HITCHING

On many islands in the Eastern Caribbean hitchhiking is the primary mode of transportation for locals. But Antigua's bus system allows for almost island wide public transportation that is quick, efficient and affordable. However, when pubic transport or finances are not available, hitching is still common and offers an adventure that exposes island life. Don't be surprised if you are standing by the roadside and someone offers you a ride; it is the island spirit to help one another. But there are also dangers as with hitchhiking anywhere in the world. Common sense and necessary precautions should be considered whenever deciding to hitch-a-ride. Women should be cautious as "negative attention" from males is notorious on the island. If you are uncomfortable with the person offering the ride, just say no thanks. Also, make sure you confirm where the person is willing to take you (although you may be surprised how people will go out of their way to make sure you arrive at your destination safely).

Hitching Like a Pro

The old stereotype of hitchhiking with your thumb in the air does not apply in Antigua. To hitch like a pro, extend your arm straight out and let your hand go limp. Let it hang there and occasionally wave down cars that look like good prospects. Couples, pick-up trucks and rental cars – tourists usually have sympathy for one another – are often good choices. You can also yell out your destination when cars pass: "Town!".

Costs and Money

For the budget and independent traveler, Antigua can seem pretty expensive. Accommodations rarely drop below US$200/night at the coastal resorts, and meals at tourist destinations average around US$10 a plate for lunch (with dinner over double the cost). But there is relief as local meals and accommodations offer island prices that can make any trip to Antigua affordable.

Exchange Rates:
1USD = 2.7EC
1GDP = 5.15EC
1EUR = 4.10EC

The currency of Antigua and Barbuda is the Eastern Caribbean dollar, which has been consistent against the U.S. dollar at 2.7 E.C. dollars. If you are planning on hitting the local shops and cafés, be sure to change your money into E.C. as local spots may not take USD. If you are staying around tourist areas and taking mainly taxis, there is no need to change your money. But buyer beware, some tourist attractions take advantage of unknowing visitors by calculating a lower exchange rate.

The best place, and really only place, to change money are at banks located in St. John's. ATMs will only dispense E.C. currency. Banks will buy back the E.C. in exchange for USD, but at your loss (banks typically buy at 2.5/6 and sell at 2.7). There are other ATMs in tourist areas such as Dickenson Bay, English Harbour and Jolly Harbour but are not reliable as it could take months for an ATM to be repaired. If you need E.C. cash, get it in St. John's before heading out exploring the island.

Credit Cards

Credit cards are widely accepted at all tourist destinations. But local spots just take cash. When traveling the island, it is a good idea to carry some E.C. currency.

TAXES

A tax of 10.5% is added to all accommodations and a 10% service charge is typically added to restaurant and hotel bills. Before leaving your tip, make sure you check the bill for this inclusion. Even the most casual places sometimes slip this in. At local joints, tipping is not expected and Antiguans rarely leave gratuity.

Antigua also has a 15% sales tax on all items purchased on the island. This, however, is not applicable to specific staple goods – like bread, rice, milk – that the government subsidizes to keep costs low. The sales tax is also not applicable to visitors at the duty-free shopping areas around Heritage Quay (pg 58).

Accommodations

While large capacity coastal resorts are numerous, Antigua has a deficit of accommodations for the independent and budget traveler. There are, however, some good choices that are usually overshadowed by large all-inclusive resorts. These smaller establishments run around US$50-100 a night and offer a Caribbean experience second to none. Many of these smaller accommodations offer lush gardens, beautiful views overlooking the Caribbean Sea, and a chance to enjoy a picturesque Caribbean holiday. Check out page 126 for realty agents specializing in villa, guesthouse and apartment rentals.

Coastal resorts are plentiful and we list many for you here (see *Accommodations* on page 122). A search on orbitz.com or expedia.com will reveal the usual suspects like Jolly Beach Resort, St. James Club or Blue Waters. If you choose to stay in a resort, there are several variables to consider:

– Do you prefer the windy and rough Atlantic Ocean or the placid Caribbean Sea?
– Is an all-inclusive resort appealing? Or would you rather explore the island?
– Do you want to experience a locally owned spot, or prefer to trust an internationally owned hotel/resort?
– When was the resort last updated? Recent renovations mean better rooms and more up-to-date services.

Food and Drink

Antiguans take their food seriously and in large portions. Local restaurants serve up traditional Caribbean cuisine that is hearty and very reasonably priced. The more tourist slanted restaurants offer comparable food, in often smaller portions, for almost double the price.

Local breakfasts are typically freshly baked baguettes filled with fish or fried egg and garnished with lettuce, tomatoes, avocado slices and other fresh vegetables. The portions are impressive for only EC$6-7. These sandwiches can usually only be purchased at roadside stands and on the streets of St. John's.

Bush Tea
Try a seeped blend of fever grass, mint leaf, and other locally picked flora - all from "the bush".

Antiguan lunch and dinner meals are quite large with mounds of rice and *ground provisions*, like cassava and dasheen. While some visitors complain about the lack of meat included with the EC$10-15 meal, West Indian diet is geared toward starches since they are less expensive and more filling. However stewed beef, jerk chicken, stewed fish and curry lamb are served in adequate portions and offer excellent Caribbean flavors. Macaroni pie (cheesy macaroni baked and sliced) and a small salad or vegetable usually accompany every meal.

Antiguan Hot Sauce

The West Indies are known for producing some of the best hot sauces in the world, and Antigua has several vying candidates. The most well known are *Susie's Hot Sauce* and *Denise's Hot Sauce*, both made with local and imported peppers. The vinegar based sauces come in a variety of flavors from volcanic temperatures to milder sauces like papaya and mango. All can be found at grocery stores for about a third of the price as a souvenir shop.

Weekend barbeques are a great way to experience Antiguan culture. On Friday and

Saturday nights, street vendors fire up their grills for an island wide cook-up offering barbequed chicken, jerk pork, ribs and anything else that can be grilled. The prices are very reasonable (a large portion of barbequed chicken runs about EC$7-10) and it is a great chance to lime with locals. In St. John's, Market Street usually has a few barbeque stands by the West Bus Station or on Independence Avenue from Nevis Street to High Street (see map on page 51).

If seafood is what you are looking for, then it's best to patron one of the higher-end restaurants. Surprisingly, local places do not serve much seafood and rarely will you find lobster except in tourist areas. During festivals and holidays, however, you can find locals grilling lobster on the street and frying fresh fish. Land crab can be found

INDEPENDENCE DAY FOOD FAIR

During independence celebrations (the week preceding Independence Day, November 1st) the Independence Day Food Fair is a great opportunity to taste an abundance of local dishes. Independence Avenue becomes crowded with vendors selling a variety of local dishes and the entire island comes out to enjoy the celebratory feast.

Some local favorites:

Ducana – A mixture of grated sweet potatoes, coconut, flour and spices wrapped in the leaf of a fig tree and boiled.

Salt Fish – Popular for local breakfast, this reconstituted dried cod is sautéed with peppers, onions, local spices and tomato sauce. Typically served with fungi.

Fungi – Brought from Africa, this dish involves "turning" cornmeal and water over a fire until it becomes firm.

Pepperpot – Beef, pork, ox tail or pig ear stewed together with dumplings or other ground provisions in a tasty, thick and sometimes spicy stew. Combined with fungi, pepperpot is the national dish of Antigua.

Roti – Curry chicken, beef or pork are seasoned and stewed before being wrapped with potatoes in a thin flour shell.

Seasoned Rice – Cooked rice specially seasoned with chunks of chicken and salted pork. A local favorite.

occasionally at street stands in St. John's. Your best bet to find this local delicacy is on Saturday mornings where a few locals sell freshly boiled crabs (EC$5-10 each) by the Public Market complex (pg 56).

Any visit to the Caribbean must include indulging in the tropical fruits and vegetables that flourish in these islands. The Public Market (pg 56) is a great place to peruse the plethora of fresh produce and there are numerous fruit stands dotting the island. Mango, papaya (called *paw paw*) and guava are all quick treats and can be purchased almost anywhere (when in season). The plantain is sliced then fried and served with breakfast or as a side dish later in the day. Breadfruit, a large dark green fruit, can be boiled to taste like a potato or roasted to bring out its flavors (some restaurants use fried breadfruit rather than French fries). Dasheen, a staple food of the Caribbean, is boiled and served as *ground provisions* with many meals. The black pineapple (pg 68), Antigua's national fruit, should not be missed. Finger rows, a small thick banana known elsewhere as *lady fingers*, are much sweeter than their larger cousin. The thin skin blackens when ripe and the fruit almost bursts out of its shell.

Antigua imports a significant amount of produce from Dominica where agriculture thrives.

Jelly

You see it all over the island in burlap bags, carts and truck-beds: green coconuts. For around EC$2-3 you can purchase one of these natural, highly nutritious refreshments right on the spot and have the top skillfully carved open, forming a spout. After finishing the drink, your vendor will slice the coconut open revealing the edible jelly inside.

Local juices include guava, mango, papaya and pineapple. When in season, the sorrel flower is boiled, strained and sweetened making a popular drink available at most local spots. Another favorite is lime squash: a mixture of lime juice and carbonated water with the occasional splash of rum.

The island offers a few domestic rums including the two most popular English Harbour and Cavalier. A unique choice is the official Kingdom of Redonda Rum, whic h is specially blended by the owner of the Bolans Village gas station. It's advertised as "perfect for punches, served neat or for cleaning automotive parts!". Sailors boast that it's the best rum on the island.

Wadadli beer advertises itself as the official beer of the island, but others such as Carib and Red Stripe offer stiff competition. These domestically brewed beers go for around EC$6 at local places with Heineken and Guinness foreign stout also available for about EC$1-2 more. For a premium, a variety of imported beers are also available.

2 for $5
Many local shops and cafés offer 2 8.75oz Wadadli beers for EC$5, called "2 for 5".

When To Go

The high season runs from mid-December through May. Typically all prices for accommodations, car rentals and airfare are at their peak during this time. If you are looking to get a deal on airfare and avoid the intense summer heat, the fall is a nice option to explore. Airlines usually offer deals for as low as US$300 from major cities in the fall (not including taxes, which will run you an additional US$120-150) and accommodations are about 20-30% cheaper. You should be aware that early fall is still the rainy season (lasting September to November) and hurricanes are possible. But rains are short-lived on the island lasting only in sudden bursts. Extended periods of rain are rare.

Some restaurants are closed during the off-season.

Staying Connected

Tri-band GSM cell phones will work via a local provider.

Internet access is wireless with pockets of service mainly around St. John's and more populated areas. Your laptop's wireless card will be able to pick up the signal from the two internet providers – Antigua Computer Technology (ACT) and Cable & Wireless – but you will not be able to access the network without authorization. You can get connected for about US$10 a day by visiting one of the companies' offices in St. John's.

Several cafés and restaurants offer free Wi-Fi access. The public library in St. John's on Market Street also has free wireless access in addition to several desktop computers. Internet cafés are available in St. John's, Jolly Harbour and English Harbour. Expect to pay about EC$5-10 for 15 minutes.

The easiest way to make phone calls home is via a Cable & Wireless prepaid card. Smartcards have a small chip that inserts into a "card" phone booth (there are "card" and "coin" phone booths, each are appropriately labeled). Smart cards come in EC$10, 20, 40, 60 and 100 denominations. A $20 Smartcard will let you talk for about 4 minutes to the U.S. or Europe.

Prepaid calling cards offer greater convenience since you can use them from any touch-tone phone. Just enter the card number and pin and the cost of the call will be deducted from the value of the card. Either type can be purchased at numerous pharmacies and shops, or at the Cable & Wireless office in St. John's.

The main post office is located on the corner of lower High Street and Thames, by Heritage Quay. There are also offices in English Harbour and Jolly Harbour.

Safety and Security

Antigua and Barbuda has seen an increase in petty crime over the last decade, infuriating many locals. Personal belongings should be monitored at all times and valuables should be kept out of sight. Violent crime, although evident on the island, is not directed towards tourists and reports of visitors being victims of violent crime is rare. With that said, normal safety precautions are advised such as walking in groups after dusk, especially in St. John's. If renting a car, be sure not to leave valuables exposed: the "R" on the license plate, for "rental", could make your vehicle a target for criminals. For more information on the current safety and security situation in Antigua, or for any travel warnings, visit: www.travel.state.gov/travel/antigua_barbuda.com

If you happen to fall ill while in Antigua, Adelin Medical Centre, just north of St. John's on Fort Road, is recommended. Holberton Hospital, the state-run public hospital, is also an option. For dental emergencies, there are numerous reputable dentists on the island.

The other concern is Antigua and Barbuda's geographic location: known as Hurricane Alley. The last hurricane to significantly impact the island was Hurricane Luis, in 1995. But every year, from September to November, Antigua and

---

HURRICANE LUIS

In September of 1995 Antigua and Barbuda received a direct hit from Hurricane Luis, a Category 4 tropical cyclone. With winds topping 140 mph and heavy rains (10 inches were recorded on Antigua), the hurricane caused an estimated US$350 million worth of damage to the twin island nation. Power outages lasted weeks and the islands' water system was severely disrupted. In addition, 3 people were killed and 165 injured. It is said that Hurricane Luis set Antigua and Barbuda back 10 years in development.

Barbuda are still at risk of receiving the wrath of these natural disasters. Contact the Office of Disaster Preparedness in case of such an emergency.

EMERGENCY CONTACT INFORMATION

Emergencies
911

Police Department
462-0125

Fire Department
462-044

Office of Disaster Preparedness
462-4402

Adelin Medical Centre
Fort Road
462-0866/7

Holberton Hospital
St. John's
462-0251

Dr. Sengupta, DDS
Woods Centre
462-9312/3

Dr. Bernard Evan-Wong, DDS
Gambles Medical Centre
462-3050

DIPLOMATIC REPRESENTATION

British High Commission
Old Parham Road
562-2124

EU Commission Office
Upper St. Georges Street
462-2970

U.S. Consular Agent
Jasmine Court
463-6531 OR 726-6531

U.S. Embassy
Bridgetown, Barbados
(246) 463-4950

Canadian High Commission
Bridgetown, Barbados
(246) 429-3550

Manchioneel Tree

Shade can be a rare commodity at some of Antigua's beaches, so a low lying, plush tree with just enough room to sit under seems like a nice option. But the Manchioneel tree (*Hippomane mancinella*) can severely irritate the skin during downpours when the sap mixes with rain and makes contact with skin. The tree is identifiable from its small, green apple-like fruits that cause severe pain and sickness if ingested. If you do make contact with the sap, rinse off the exposed area immediately.

ST. JOHN'S

Introduction

Every morning the villages nearly drain as islanders make their way towards St. John's, or "Town" as it is commonly known, the island's commercial center. Almost all government ministries are located here and with the government employing about 35% of the population, many Antiguans have found employment in the capital. In addition, St. John's accommodates several banks, office buildings and retail stores including Heritage Quay, Redcliffe Quay and the more locally oriented Market Street.

The Ministry of Tourism promotes the National Museum of Antigua and Barbuda and St. John's Cathedral as major tourist attractions. These sites should not be overlooked, but St. John's also offers the opportunity to experience one of the best Caribbean capital cities while exploring local hang-outs, sampling the local cuisine, and absorbing some of the Antiguan culture.

ORIENTATION

St. John's main drag is Market Street stretching from the West Bus Station north to High Street. If St. John's had a major intersection, High Street and Market Street would be it. From High Street east to Independence Ave is another busy stretch. West from High Street and Market Street is the main tourist area, Heritage Quay, where cruise ship passengers disembark to explore the island. Here you will find duty-free shopping and several trendy clothing outlets (not to mention the throngs of taxi drivers and street vendors). Redcliffe Quay is a beautifully restored area nestled by the docks of St. John's. Once the slave market and rum distillery, Redcliffe Quay is now top real estate for restaurants and souvenir boutiques.

GETTING AROUND

The sidewalks in St. John's have recently been renovated after years of neglect. They are now wider and more accessible.

There is no bus service within St. John's but luckily you really don't need any transportation other than your feet. Set in a grid system, the 4 square miles of the capital are easy to navigate. If, however, you would like a lift, taxis are readily available from about EC$15 to take you anywhere within the city.

If you drive to the capital parking can be a problem, especially during weekday business hours. There is a secure car park on lower Newgate Street charging EC$2/hour or EC$12/day. A multistory car park is currently under construction near the East Bus Station. Alternatively, you can vie for a street parking space, which are free of charge, but can be difficult to find. You should keep in mind that illegal parking in the capital is finable and tickets are regularly issued by the police.

Sites

1. National Museum of Antigua and Barbuda
2. St. John's Cathedral
3. Government House
4. Antigua Recreation Grounds
5. Cenotaph
6. East Bus Station
7. Botanical Gardens
8. Country Pond
9. V.C. Bird Monment
10. Market Complex
11. West Bus Station
12. Heritage Quay
13. Redcliffe Quay

Resources

14. ACT Office (Inside Radioshack)
15. Cable & Wireless Office
16. Police Headquarters
➕ Pharmacy
✉ Post Office
$ Bank/ATM
P Parking
⋯⋯ Suggested Walking Tour

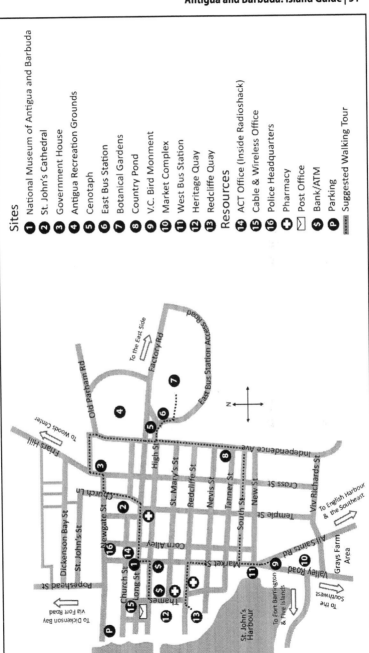

Sights

ST. JOHN'S CATHEDRAL

Looming over the capital for which it takes its name, St. John's Cathedral is an impressive sight. The current structure is actually the third and most elaborate church to be constructed on this hill overlooking the city. An earthquake in 1683 destroyed a small wooden church that sat on this site and in 1843 another quake caused severe damage to a larger brick cathedral. The designers of the current structure wanted to ensure that history would not repeat itself, so a pitch pine interior was created encasing the freestone structure to provide protection from earthquakes and hurricanes. This design has caused the cathedral to be called "a church within a church".

Today the cathedral has fallen into disrepair and a restoration project has been in the works for several years. Despite the needed repairs, the cathedral offers regular service for the public and is open for all to visit. The large cemetery with wide horizontal headstones has turned into a picnic area for Antiguan workers on their lunch breaks – during a hot afternoon the cathedral's elevated status provides a much needed breeze above the city. It is not uncommon to find the graveyard crowded with locals cooling out over the crumbling graves of early colonizers.

WAR RELICS

Two figures, cast in lead and covered in white wash, rest above the southern entrance. These figures represent St. John the Baptist and St. John the Devine and are said to have been captured from a French ship in the Caribbean Sea destined for Martinique during the Seven Years War.

NATIONAL MUSEUM OF ANTIGUA & BARBUDA
MARKET STREET AND LONG STREET; 462-1469
MON-FRI 8:30AM-4PM, SAT 10AM-2PM; US$3/EC$8, 12 AND UNDER FREE

This small yet informative museum gives a brief historical overview of the island. Although many of the exhibits seem outdated, the museum gives the visitor a better understanding of the island's history. Of special interest are the early photographs on display and additional archived photos.

Check out the out-of-place hippopotamus skull.

The museum opened in 1985 in what was once the old St. John's Court House, constructed in 1750. Today it is operated by the Historical & Archeological Society, a private non-profit organization, which also hosts several historical seminars and events that are open to the public. Inquire with the museum for further information.

Find More...
ON THE WEB
www.antiguamuseums.org

GOVERNMENT HOUSE
NEWGATE STREET AND CROSS STREET
NOT OPEN TO THE PUBLIC

Built around 1750 and occupied at the time by the well known merchant Thomas Norbury Kerby, this residence was purchased by the British government in 1807 as the official house for the Governor of the Leeward Islands. Although 35 Governor Generals have lived here, the most revered was Governor Oliver Baldwin who promoted social and economic reform to improve the lives of black Antiguans. Due to these controversial views of the time, Baldwin was recalled to England in 1950 after only a short two year post and subsequently died in 1958. Upon his request, Baldwin's ashes were buried in Antigua on Green Castle Hill (pg 62).

ANTIGUAN RECREATION GROUNDS (ARG)
FACTORY ROAD AND INDEPENDENCE AVENUE

The ARG was once the national venue for all entertainment and sporting events, including the beloved West Indies Cricket. Chikie's HiFi in the party stand and Sir Viv's record breaking moments have enshrined the ARG in Antiguan history. Today the venue has been overshadowed by the new Sir Vivian Richards Stadium (pg 82), which was built in preparation for the 2007 Cricket World Cup and many believe will eventually replace the ARG. To the elation of Antiguans with fond memories of the ARG, events are still held here. For more information on upcoming events, call ☎462-1419.

Food and beverage stalls located inside the ARG are open Mon-Sat during lunch hours.

CENOTAPH
FACTORY ROAD AND INDEPENDENCE AVENUE

Located on Independence Ave, between the ARG and East Bus Station, is Antigua and Barbuda's memorial to those Antiguans and Barbudans who lost their lives serving in the First and Second World Wars. Each year on Remembrance Day a ceremony is held at the monument and wreaths are placed around the memorial.

East Bus Station
FACTORY ROAD AND INDEPENDENCE AVENUE

The East Bus Station is where locals go to lime after working hours (or during, for that matter) while playing dominoes at Obie's bar or eating local meals from the numerous food stalls. During Carnival (pg 29) an unofficial "shantytown" is erected.

HER MAJESTY'S PRISON

Behind the ARG is Antigua's prison known as "1735" after the date of its construction (evident on the arch entrance). The prison houses nearly 200 inmates who work the grounds at the ARG and even sell handmade crafts outside the West Bus Station – look for them in the all white jumpsuits.

BOTANICAL GARDENS
LOCATED ON THE EAST BUS STATION ACCESS ROAD
OPEN MON-SUN 7:00AM-7:00PM; FREE ADMISSION

After originally opening in 1888, these gardens went through a century of neglect until the newly appointed Prime Minister Baldwin Spencer declared they would be among the greatest in the world. They haven't quite reached that stage, but the government has put a tremendous amount of effort into developing a relaxing and lush environment for locals and tourists alike. A great place to enjoy a quiet picnic is under the impressive African Zulu tree located near the entrance. Picnic tables are available under the enormous tree and at various locations throughout the 6 acre garden.

ST. JOHN'S MEDICAL CENTRE
QUEEN ELIZABETH HIGHWAY

Sitting atop Mt. St. John's, just up Queen Elizabeth Highway, is the impressive US$50 million medical facility that was completed in 2003 to replace the aging Holberton Hospital as Antigua's main medical care center. The state-of-the-art facility was funded with the assistance of foreign governments and a hefty donation from Allen Stanford. Unfortunately the hospital is yet to be operational as the government has struggled to fulfill staffing and budgetary requirements.

COUNTRY POND
INDEPENDENCE AVE AND NEVIS ST

Formerly called Congo Pond after the enslaved Congolese who reportedly built this small reservoir in the mid-1800s, Country Pond was once St. John's only fresh water source. In 2004 the newly appointed government commissioned a Haitian immigrant to compose the mural on the far wall depicting pre- and post-colonial Antigua.

V.C. BIRD MONUMENT
MARKET STREET, VALLEY ROAD AND ALL SAINTS ROAD

Impossible to ignore, this massive bronze bust of V.C. Bird is located just outside the Public Market at the intersection of Market Street, Valley Road and All Saints Road. Unveiled in 1987, it recently received improvements with fresh paint and a newly designed area encasing the monument.

MARKET COMPLEX
MARKET STREET, VALLEY ROAD AND ALL SAINTS ROAD
MON-SAT 7:00AM-6:00PM, SAT 5:30AM-6:00PM

The best time to visit the public market is on Saturday morning when vendors from around the island pour into the capital with fruits, vegetables and anything else that might sell. The market opens around 5:30am and lasts well into the afternoon. You'll find a plethora of local produce and if you aren't sure what something is, just ask the vendor who is usually happy to assist.

The adjoining Craft Market was designed to allow local artisans a place to craft and sell their works. Unfortunately, the present market doesn't have much in terms of local crafts to offer

INSIGHT·

Gray's Farm

South of the Market Complex is an area known as Gray's Farm, the poorest residential area on the island. In recent years the community has seen a significant influx of Dominican immigrants bringing a vibrant culture that complements the Caribbean atmosphere. There are several local establishments serving ice cold Presidentes (the popular Dominican beer) and empanadas straight from a Latino kitchen. Sunday afternoons are especially lively as the small drinking establishments fill up.

While keeping normal safety considerations in mind (see page 47), exploring the area during the day is relatively safe. Although, due to the extreme poverty of the community, extra precautions should be taken after dusk. Petty theft is common and shootings have been reported.

Across the street, next to the West Bus Station, you'll find the fisheries complex. Everyday local fishermen bring their fresh catch to the complex for public sale. The daily catch varies, but you can usually find snapper, wahoo, king fish, conch and sometimes lobster. You can walk to the back of the complex to see the fishermen cleaning their boats, hand-making lobster cages, or just liming with a game of dominoes.

Shopping

MARKET STREET
SHOPS OPEN MON-SAT 9:00AM-6:00PM

Market Street is where locals go to shop. Almost all of the stores are owned and operated by Middle Eastern families that have immigrated to Antigua and the items they sell are typically western and modern in style. If you are looking to get a bargain deal on some souvenirs, like a West Indies Cricket jersey, you can find it here for half the price of a tourist shop in Heritage Quay.

SHOUL'S
MON-SAT 9:00AM-6:00PM

Stephen B. Shoul may be the Sam Walton of Antigua. He opened his first department store in the 1980s and has since opened three more offering everyday items, housewares and clothing. All at rock-bottom prices. You can find three of his stores on Market Street and another on Newgate Street.

REDCLIFFE QUAY
MON-SAT 9:00AM-6:00PM

Just to the south of Heritage Quay and tucked behind a row of shops on Redcliffe Street, this area was once the island's main trading venue for slaves, rum and sugar. Today, Redcliffe Quay has been beautifully restored featuring vibrant Georgian architecture in a tropical environment. Shops, cafés and restaurants have replaced the trading grounds of colonial Antigua, but the atmosphere still has a sense of history.

BEST OF BOOKS/MADE IN ANTIGUA
MON-SAT 9:00AM-5:30PM

This two-in-one store offers a wide variety of literature from today's bestsellers, to unique Caribbean works by local writers. Made in Antigua, in a small nook in the back of Best of Books, is a rare outlet for local artisans wanting to market and sell their craft.

HERITAGE QUAY
MON-SAT 9:00AM-6:00PM

This is the quintessential cruise ship port. Everyday during high season, thousands of visitors crowd Heritage Quay where duty-free shops and upscale souvenir stores are housed in a massive outdoor complex.

THE SOUTHWEST

Introduction

The southwest has a Caribbean flare and lively atmosphere infusing the villages there with life. Expatriates have recently started migrating to the area after discovering the relatively low rent and colorful villages (with ample rum shops). But the villages have kept their local charm and are adjusting well to the transplanted residents.

This area is also Antigua's most fertile region with its black pineapple farms and mango trees around every corner. Mango season begins in June and the villages soon become inundated with the sweet fruit.

Beaches, beaches and more beaches...
If you are interested in an almost never ending beach, then you have come to the right place as some of Antigua's best beaches are located in an area starting at Jolly Harbour and continuing to Old Road Village, a stretch known as *Round South*. With one beautiful beach after another, a visitor can beach hop with ease.

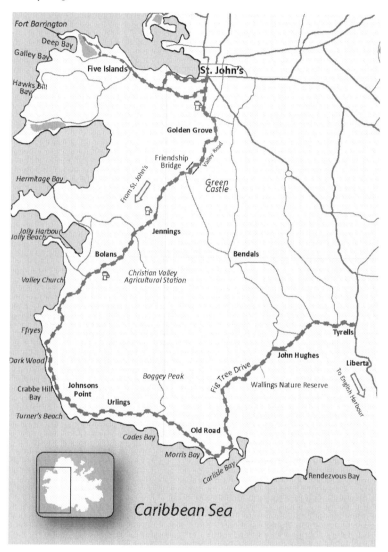

ORIENTATION

On your way out of St. John's, you may consider turning right after the West Bus Station and head towards Five Islands Village, Fort Barrington and Deep Bay. After exploring this western outlet, head south towards *Round South*. On the way, there is a hike to Green Castle Hill just outside Jennings Village that offers great views over the island. Christian Valley Agricultural Station, with orchards of tropical fruit trees, is definitely worth the trip. Then, after Jolly Harbour, continue through the stretches of beach until Old Road and the tropical Fig Tree Drive.

Getting Around
Sample taxi rates (USD, one-way, 4 persons) from St. John's to:

Jolly Harbour $18
Johnsons Point $22
Old Road $26

Bus routes from St. John's (West Bus Station):

#20: Golden Grove, Jennings, Bolans, Jolly Harbour
#22: Continues to Johnsons Point, Urlings, Old Road

Sights

FORT BARRINGTON
The smooth main road leading from St. John's turns into a rough, pothole riddled path leading to this small fort.

Park in the small car park and cross the adjacent bridge before reaching a trail leading up Goat Hill.

Originally used as a signal station reporting ship movements via flag and light signals, Fort Barrington was captured by the French in 1666 only to be recaptured by the British a year later. In 1779 Admiral Barrington, for whom the fort is named, greatly increased the structure's fortifications to fend off enemy ships from entering St. John's harbor. The fort offers impressive views over St. John's and the turquoise laden Deep Bay.

DEEP BAY AND THE ANDES SHIPWRECK
Follow the path down Goat Hill from Fort Barrington and take a right. A small trail through 10-15 yards of bush will lead you to Deep Bay and its long stretch of white sand beach. At the far end is the Royal Antiguan Hotel and out in the water,

resting in just 30 feet of water, lies the Andes shipwreck.

The Andes set sail from Trinidad on 5 June 1905 with 1,330 barrels of asphalt bound for Valparaiso. The Andes stopped in Antigua and when local authorities opened the hatch to inspect the cargo, the sudden air caused the vessel to catch fire, eventually sinking the ship. Today, over a hundred years later, the Andes sits at the bottom of the bay for scuba divers and snorkelers to explore.

Five Islands Area

It is easy to find yourself casually exploring this western peninsula while taking in the local atmosphere and sites. Small fruit stands, local shops and stray cattle are all apparent here, along with the notable Galley Bay and Hawksbill Beach, named after the rock formation off its shores. All are worthy of your time (well maybe not the roaming cattle).

GREEN CASTLE HILL

 DRIVING DIRECTIONS To head south to further sites, turn back towards Valley Road and take a right, leading through Golden Grove and Jennings Village.

Beginning at the northern tip of Jennings, to the left immediately after crossing Friendship Bridge, is the beginning of a 45 minute hike to Green Castle Hill. Offering superb views over the surrounding landscape, this 565ft vista is the remnant of an isolated volcano that some believe was once the site of ancient pagan rituals as megaliths, or arrangements of small boulders, can be found on the southwestern summit. There is also a large stone plaque where the ashes of Lord Baldwin, the beloved Governor of the Leeward Islands (see Government House on page 53) are interred. An inscription on his plaque reads: "He loved the people of these islands".

HERMITAGE BAY

You may be wondering where you are going as you dodge stray pigs and cows on the dirt road that leads to one of our favorite beaches, Hermitage Bay. Located down a dirt road at the southern end of Jennings, this beach has recently se en the development of a first class resort, Hermitage Bay Hotel (pg 124). But public parking is still available and the beach is open for all to enjoy. Head north, right when facing the water, to escape the resort's territory and find pristine swimming conditions that are almost always empty.

TIP Hermitage Bay is a great spot for beach combing as the shore is littered with sea shells.

CHRISTIAN VALLEY AGRICULTURAL STATION

You won't find a lot of tourists roaming through the fruit orchards or climbing up to the top of a mango tree for that perfectly ripe treat, but this sprawling 40 acre produce plantation wedged inside the Sherkely Mountains is definitely worth a visit. You can buy fresh produce by the dozen or simply roam through the pastures, each categorized by a particular fruit: guava, breadfruit, avocado, mango and soursop (just to name a few). During mango season, check out the 25 different types of mangoes like the giant *kite* and the popular *kidney*.

The entrance to Christian Valley, on the left, is clearly marked.

JOLLY HARBOUR

Behind the security fences and concrete walls you'll find a prefabricated community of expatriates and tourists. Although that's not a bad thing, especially if you are missing the modern conveniences of life back home. The Epicurean, a modern and well stocked grocery store, is located here along with a few drinking spots (favorites of resident sailors) decorated with all the pirate fixins. Jolly Beach is full of activity and local vendors will sell you anything from beach chair rentals to pirated DVDs.

DRIVING DIRECTIONS To access the beach, turn right off the main road after passing Bolans Village, take the first right and then an immediate left. Follow the road past a small security post to Castaways Restaurant car park.

Gladiators Casino

The first thing you notice when turning into Jolly Harbour is this large casino. Imagination lends you to believe it is full of wealthy travelers and expatriates enthralled in high-stakes gambling. But when you open the doors you are surprised to find it empty, completely empty. On rare occasions a rouge tourist or local kid may pop tokens into the slot machines, but the rest of the time its void of life. If you are looking play some roulette or blackjack, however, the casino does have the employees to indulge you.

ISLANDS OFF THE SOUTHWEST COAST

The views from the southwest are nothing short of spectacular. In case you are wondering just what those islands are off in the distance, here is a brief summary:

Montserrat

In July 1995 the Soufriere Hills Volcano, which had been dormant for 400 years, suddenly erupted on Montserrat, burying the island's capital of Plymouth. The entire southern side of the island was destroyed and declared an Exclusion Zone, forbidding entry at any time. Luckily there were no deaths involved but of the 10,000 people living on Montserrat at the time, over 7,000 fled. Many of whom were warmly welcomed on Antigua as the two islands share a common history and culture.

ANTIGUA'S MANGO FESTIVAL

In 2006 Christian Valley hosted Antigua's first Mango Festival, which has since become a yearly occurrence every July. The event is strongly supported locally with live music, an abundance of local food, and enough mangoes to fill the most gluttonous appetite. For more information, go to www.antiguamangofest.com.

Today the volcano has significantly subsided but it is still active and on clear days the summit can be seen from Antigua's southern shores.

Redonda

When Columbus passed this small isle, which measures barely a square mile, on 11 November 1493, he quickly named it Santa Maria la Redonda after a chapel in Cadiz. Columbus declared the isle inaccessible and it remained uninhabited for nearly 400 years until a worldwide demand for calcium phosphate erupted in the mid-1800s. It so happened that Redonda was inundated in the chemically rich bird guano. A later discovery of aluminum phosphate beneath the guano spurred the interest of an American company that would eventually haul off thousands of tons of phosphate.

The once prosperous phosphate industry dwindled in response to shipping problems associated with the First World War (Germany happened to be the American company's biggest client). The entire operation ceased in 1929 after a hurricane destroyed much of the already deteriorated equipment and infrastructure.

The isle remains uninhabited today, except for several species of fauna including a marooned herd of sheep and the burrowing owl (which, like the Antigua Racer snake, became extinct on Antigua after the mongoose was introduced). Adventurous sailors continue to make occasional pilgrimages to Redonda, but few actually step foot on its shores as the rough seas and unwelcoming port make it difficult to access.

Kingdom of Redonda

On a blistery day in May of 1998, Robert Williamson set sail from Antigua with 65 "loyal subjects" to claim the kingdom of Redonda. Williamson and his crew navigated a 130ft topsail schooner through the treacherous waters and safely landed on the island where they planted a banal flag while Williamson crowned himself King Robert the Bald. He was not the first, however, as a long line of "Kings" have staked their title on the uninhabited rock. Some have received official decrees from the Crown in England, while others have simply declared themselves the rightful heir to the island.

SOUTHWEST BEACHES

Leaving Jolly Harbour and heading southeast, you enter beach country. The beaches along this stretch owe much of their fame to the gentle Caribbean Sea that graces their shores and the crystal clear water it brings. The views of Redonda, Nevis, smoldering Montserrat and, on especially clear days, Guadeloupe only add to the area's appeal. Here is a quick rundown from north to southeast:

TIP To access these beaches using public transport, take the #22 bus that runs from St. John's to Old Road.

Valley Church

Nice long stretch of white sand with plenty of natural shade. Can get crowded on Sunday when the U.S. Air Station (pg 94) hosts its weekly picnic with locals joining in.

Ffryes

One of Antigua's best kept secret, Ffryes gets packed on holiday weekends when locals throw beach bashes on this long desolate beach. The rest

DIPLOMATIC IMMUNITY?

In 2007 a pub in Southhampton England attempted to gain diplomatic immunity from a nationwide ban on smoking in pubs by establishing themselves as the official Embassy of Redonda in Britain. Sir Robert the Bald sent a special emissary, Redonda's official Cardinal, to knight the establishment's owner and open Redonda's first embassy. The British Foreign Office, however, rejected the claim as Redonda is a territory of Antigua and Barbuda, not a sovereign nation.

of the year, this pristine beach is empty. The one drawback is lack of shelter, but Dennis' Restaurant (pg 118) is just a short walk away offering fantastic views.

Darkwood

Nestled at the foot of a steep hill and with crystal clear water this beach is, as one local explained, "the best". It lost some of its long beach to Hurricane Luis but managed to keep its charm.

Turner's Beach

Never empty yet rarely packed, Turner's is a subdued version of Jolly Beach with vendors selling fresh aloe for sun-burnt skin and water sport rentals are readily available. Shelter is available on a first come basis.

Cades Bay

If you are looking for a bit of snorkeling, then this is the beach for you. You can explore by yourself, or hire a boat to take you to the 2.5 mile long Cades Reef to see an abundance of marine life.

Morris Bay

Local residents from Old Road frequent this beach as an alternative to the more uppity Carlisle Bay. Colorful fishing boats are scattered across the shores with fishermen telling tales of the one that got away.

BOGGEY PEAK

Visitors are almost always disappointed when they reach the highest point on Antigua (1,319ft). Instead of the breathtaking views across the Caribbean Sea and the feeling of accomplishment, they find an obscured view by less than attractive shrubbery. The communications company Cable & Wireless promptly planted a massive antenna and security fence on Boggey Peak, obstructing the view. But if you contact the company (☎480-4000), they will work with you to arrange a time for access into the secured area from which you can take in the views on top of Antigua's highest point.

OLD ROAD

Established in 1632, Old Road is the oldest village on Antigua. The village seems alive with children playing barefoot and brightly colored chattel houses lining the streets. People here appear a bit friendlier, the foliage a little more verdant, and the paint shines brighter on the colorful homes. You can check out St. Mary's Church, which is the oldest church on the island, or enjoy some fresh fish on Morris Bay. The sunsets on Carlisle Bay aren't half bad either.

The Black Pineapple

This sweet treat, that is considered a specialty of Antigua, not to mention the national fruit, can be found growing throughout the area around Old Road. The black pineapple (*Ananas Comosus)* takes its name from the dark color of its infancy which turns yellow when ripened.

You can purchase a neatly sliced pineapple (for eating on the spot) at several roadside fruit stands around Old Road and John Hughes Village. Expect to pay between EC$12-15 for a cut and prepared pineapple, or even less when buying at the Public Market (pg 56) in St. John's.

Stop by Claremont Farms just outside Old Road to see a pineapple farm first hand.

FIG TREE DRIVE

Named for the banana fields that line this stretch of road, Fig Tree Drive cuts through Antigua's only rainforest. The road itself has seen extensive repairs over the last few years and what was once inaccessible, now offers a smooth, wide surface to cruise along while taking in the tropical scenery. Rainforest Canopy Tours (pg 101) has zip line tours offering impressive bird's eye views while you zing along between tree platforms. If you want to try some of the area's fresh produce, stop by The

Culture Shop (☎460-3949) which has been selling local jams, hot sauces, seasonal fruits and souvenirs for fifteen years.

Fig Tree Studio Art Gallery

Tucked just off Fig Tree Drive is a small art gallery featuring works of local and regional artists. The studio is owned by a mother and daughter who also reside on the property; much of what is displayed is their work.

WALLINGS RESERVOIR NATURE RESERVE

If you are looking to keep your feet on the ground and still enjoy the area, then head up to Wallings Nature Reserve situated off Fig Tree Drive on the right (when traveling north from Old Road) in the heart of the forest. The reservoir was built around 1900 and was designed to hold 13 million gallons of water for supplying fifteen surrounding villages. In 1912, after three years of drought, the reservoir was drained and a systematic reforestation project around the structure began. The innovative plan called for planting trees on 13 acres of surrounding land. The trees would absorb and eventual release water, making the area a lush, moist woodland.

Today, the area is a nature reserve with picnic tables and hiking trails. The remnants of the Victorian industrial design of the reservoir still exist adding contrast to the natural environment engulfing it.

THE SOUTHEAST

Introduction

The biggest attractions to this part of the island are English and Falmouth Harbours, the historic Nelson's Dockyard, and Shirley's Heights with its Sunday afternoon barbeque with breathtaking views. English Harbour is filled with a Caribbean atmosphere accentuated by brightly colored homes, restaurants and cafés. Pigeon Beach provides a nice swimming spot that gets crowded with English Harbour residents and the restaurants and nightlife of the area make it a great place to spend an evening. Stroll through the docks at Falmouth Harbour, especially during Sailing Week, to check out the assortment of sailboats and multimillion dollar yachts.

The first free settlement after emancipation, Liberta, is located on the way to the harbours, along with several other worthy sites including Great George Fort.

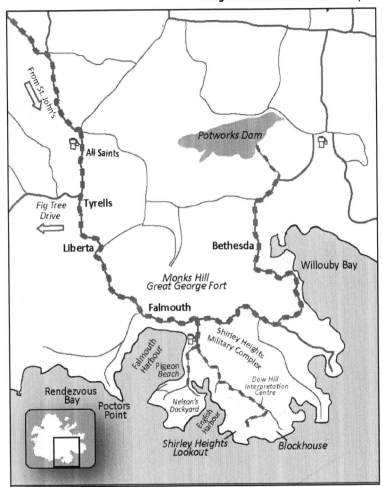

ORIENTATION

From St. John's, take the All Saints Road that runs through All Saints, Tyrells and Liberta before reaching Falmouth Harbour. Ample parking is available just outside Nelson's Dockyard and the area is easily explored on foot. Transportation is required, however, to visit the Interpretation Centre and Shirley Heights Military Complex. When leaving the harbors, head towards Potworks Dam and Bethesda.

Getting Around

Sample taxi rates (USD, one-way, 4 persons) from St. John's to:

All Saints $13
Lberta $19
Nelson's Dockyard $25

Bus routes from St. John's (West Bus Station):

#15: All Saints, Tyrells, Liberta
#17:Continues to Falmouth, Nelson's Dockyard

Sights

POTTERY IN SEA VIEW FARM

A short drive off All Saints Road brings you to the village of Sea View Farm. The community is home to Elvie's Pottery, one of the last vestiges of Antigua's pottery industry that once flourished in this village. Elvie passed away in 1987 and since then her daughter, Hyacinth Hillmore, has been carrying out the craft in a small cramped shop adjacent to her home. Today the visitor is welcome to stop by the little shop and watch as local clay is used to hand mold coal pots, bowls and pitchers.

ALL SAINTS VILLAGE

From Sea View Farm turn back to All Saints Road and head for the village for which the main road takes its name, All Saints. The largest settlement after St. John's on Antigua, All Saints is where the parishes of St. John's, St. George, St. Peter, St. Phillip's and St. Mary's all meet. Hence the name: All Saints.

TYRELLS

 Turn right at the gas station in All Saints and continue straight until you reach the village of Tyrells.

Tyrells is a sleepy village nestled between All Saints, Swetes and Liberta. The village is named after Captain Richard Tyrell who, in 1766, became the Commander-in-Chief of the Dockyard and later purchased the estate that is Tyrells today.

There are a couple of interesting spots in Tyrells, with the first catching almost everyone's eye and the other is a bit harder to see. *Our Lady of Perpetual Help* is a beautiful pink church resting on a small hill that is almost impossible to ignore. Built in 1932, the size, architecture and color of this Roman Catholic Church adds a splash of grandeur to an otherwise unexciting scenery.

Just down the road from the pink church and off to the left is *The Boat House*. This interesting home was built in 1972 in the shape of a boat's hull by the current resident Sonny Gore and his wife. Sonny worked for a British construction firm in St. John's during the 1960s where he honed his drafting skills. Putting these skills into practice, Sonny built his home to "suit the land" after it became wedged during the construction of the All Saints Road in 1969. Today the house is in stark contrast to the surrounding traditional West Indian homes.

LIBERTA

Continuing on All Saints Road, immediately past Tyrells, is the first free village on Antigua.

Shortly following emancipation in 1835, an estate owner, for financial reasons, sold off the property in small lots. Nearby black laborers working on plantations or as mechanics at the dockyard, quickly bought the land. A small settlement began and for the first time free blacks owned their own property. They suitably called this community Liberta.

STIGMATA

In 1998 Father Gerard Critch of Our Lady of Perpetual Help began having severe pain in his side, hands and feet. When blood began to ooze from his wrist and ankles, he claimed to be the recipient of stigmata. Parishioners who touched Father Critch reportedly buckled to the floor or miraculously had ailments healed. After unsuccessful medical treatment in Antigua, Allen Stanford flew the priest to New York on a private jet to be treated by church specialists.

GREAT GEORGE FORT

Horseback Riding
Spring Hill Riding Club (pg 102) offers horseback excursions up Monk's Hill to explore Great George Fort.

Behind Falmouth, resting on the 588ft Monk's Hill, is the Great George Fort. Construction of the fort began in 1689 and and was designed to be the last refuge for island colonizers in the event of a French or Carib attack. In 1712 women and children were ordered to the fortification as a French attack was believed to be imminent. The attack, however, never occurred.

Today the fort can be explored on foot through an arched entrance in the northern end of a stone wall encircling the 8 acres of land holding the barracks, gun sites, hospital and water cisterns. The view is quite impressive and one can see why the site was chosen as an ideal location for surveying the island.

FALMOUTH HARBOUR

Falmouth Harbour is notable for the number and size of the yachts that dock here. From cruising sailboats to multimillion dollar luxury yachts, Falmouth has hosted the finest ships from around the world and can become a prime docking

YACHTY ME BE!

A yachty is a career sailor who is crew-for-hire on luxury boats, racing sailboats, or is simply recruited by a wealthy boat owner to care for a ship. Sailing around the world can be exhausting business, so when they are in port they know how to party and spend money making English Harbour an oasis for the weary sailor. The bars and restaurants here are well equipped to keep these thirsty and hungry sailors content.

location during high season. As a visitor, you can walk around the docks to get a first hand glimpse of these magnificent ships. The harbor also has several small shops and cafés to enjoy.

NELSON'S DOCKYARD

DAILY 9:00AM-5:00PM
EC$15, INCLUDES ADMISSION INTO THE INTERPRETATION CENTER AND DOCKYARD MUSEUM

The construction of Her Majesty's Antigua Naval Yard began in 1725 as a repair station for the Royal Navy Warships required to protect and strengthen Britain's imperial assets in the Eastern Caribbean. The location proved ideal as a natural bastion against damaging hurricanes and with Britain erecting fortifications guarding its entrance, the harbor became impenetrable for enemy ships. During its peak the harbor enlisted 5 British officers and 327 men, most of whom were enslaved Africans

TIP There is ample free parking just outside the dockyard.

The harbor became less important after the 1815 peace accords and officially closed in 1889. It wasn't until 1951 when the then Governor General established the Friends of English Harbour Society that any serious restoration efforts began. Since that time, Nelson's Dockyard – named after its most famous resident and commander, Horatio Nelson – has received substantial support from the Canadian Government, the British Government and the European Union. Today it is under the auspices of the National Parks Authority and is Antigua's most impressive historical site.

Find More...
ON THE WEB
www.antiguamuseums.org

DOCKYARD MUSEUM

OPEN DAILY, 9:00AM-5:00PM
FREE WITH ADMISSION INTO THE DOCKYARD

This museum inside the Naval Officer's House retells the story of the Dockyard dating back nearly a millennia to its first inhabitants up to recent restorations and modern day sailing ships.

Most of the museum, however, is focused on the time when the dockyard was careening and outfitting British warships and tells a unique history of the English conquest for domination in the Caribbean, slavery, King Sugar and life on the island.

FORT BERKELEY

A short walk behind the Dockyard, sitting on a peninsula forming the west entrance to the harbor, rests Fort Berkeley. Construction began in 1704, 21 years before the Dockyard was built, as the first line of defense at English Harbour. You will notice an upturned cannon cemented in the rock at the end of the fort. This once connected a chain that extended to Fort Charlotte – now only a pile of rubble – across the harbor forming a boom to discourage enemy ships.

PIGEON BEACH

In Antigua you are never far from a beach and English Harbour is no exception. With boats anchored off its shores, Pigeon Beach can get crowded with English Harbour residents on the weekends (especially on Sunday before everyone heads to Shirley Heights). Picnic benches with plenty of shade are available as well as locals selling barbeque on the weekend.

CLARENCE HOUSE

Head out of English and Falmouth Harbours and take a right towards Shirley Heights. Travel up a steep hill and around a couple bends until you will see the Clarence House on the right.

Princess Margaret spent her honeymoon at Clarence House.

Built in 1787 for the Duke of Clarence, who would later became King William IV, this Georgian style house was used as a country home for the governors of the Leeward Islands. Unfortunately,

Hurricane Luis severely damaged the structure in 1995 but it has since received repairs.

DOW'S HILL INTERPRETATION CENTRE
OPEN DAILY, 9:00AM-5:00PM
FREE WITH ADMISSION INTO THE DOCKYARD

The Interpretation Centre's 15 minute presentation covering the history of Antigua is disappointing for anyone looking for substantive information on the subject (the presentation, whether intentional or not, appears to be intended for children). The biggest draw to this site is the location. Dow's Hill, named after General Alexander Dow whose house once stood on this site, offers notable views of the surrounding area. If you are lucky and the guides are in the mood, you might get a brief tour of the area included with your admission. Inquire at the main desk for details.

SHIRLEY HEIGHTS MILITARY COMPLEX

Take a left after leaving the Interpretation Centre and you will, without noticing, enter the Shirley Heights Military Complex. The area was named after Sir Thomas Shirley, Governor of the Leeward Islands from 1781 to 1788, who strengthened Antigua's defenses in response to Britain's dwindling control over the West Indies. He needed to ensure Antigua's sugar production and the ever important Dockyard were well protected from foreign powers. Today, the complex is best known for the views offered from the Blockhouse and the crowded Sunday afternoon barbeque that has become Antigua's best known party.

The Blockhouse

Keep to the left at the fork in the road that leads to the Blockhouse on top of Cape Shirley, Antigua's most southerly point. You will notice the ruins of the Officer's Quarters and a small cemetery which is the final resting place for many early settlers. Although not much of the historical value of this location has been preserved, the views over Mamora Bay, and Eric Clapton's palatial estate (to the east) are worth a short trip.

The Lookout

Be sure to arrive early to enjoy the sunset.

Shirley Heights is synonymous with the Sunday barbeque that is filled with live music, plenty of drinks, great food and a picturesque view of the setting sun over English Harbour (every Sunday from 4pm-11pm, admission EC$25, free parking). The atmosphere is relaxed with locals, expats and tourists mingling while sipping rum punch or a Wadadli. A full steel pan band entertains guests until a local soca/reggae group takes over. It is a must during any trip to Antigua.

RENDEZVOUS BAY

Due to its remote location, plan to spend at least 2 hours here.

Rendezvous Bay is one of the most difficult beaches to reach on the island due to the seriously poor condition of the road that leads to it. But if you can make the trek (in which a four-wheel drive vehicle is recommended) the beach is pristine. You can also drive part way and then walk for about 30 minutes. Another option to reach this secluded beach is to hire a water taxi in Falmouth Harbour (usually departing from Pigeon Beach) for the short trip around Poctors Point.

TAMARIND TREE

A tamarind tree in Bethesda is one of Antigua's most important yet unspectacular historical landmarks. It was here, under this tree in 1951, that V.C. Bird and his Antigua Trades and Labour Union stood up to Alexander Moody-Stuart, the sugar mogul, demanding better pay rates. Dressed in his usual white suit and seated on his horse above the workers, Mr. Moody-Stuart urged the workers to go back to the fields and resume their labor or face starvation. The workers refused stating that they would survive by picking the widdy-widdy bush and collecting cockles until a fair payment scheme was met. Without pay they survived the long strike and on 2 Jan 1952 the workers received a 25% pay increase. The ATLU would continue to gain political power, eventually forming the Antigua Labour Party that would dominate the Antigua political arena until 2004.

POTWORKS DAM

Reputed to be the largest freshwater reservoir in the Eastern Caribbean, this 320 acre basin holds 1 billion gallons of water. Held by the Potworks Dam to the east and the Delaps Dam to the south with the former being the largest, this reservoir is named after an 18th century pottery works owned by the Codrington family. The construction of the dam began in the 1960s and on the eve of completion the dam surprisingly filled to capacity after an above average rainy season.

Bird Watching
The freshwater attracts several species of birds including the rare West Indian whistling duck.

THE EAST

Introduction

The east side is considerably less developed than the other areas of the island. Long stretches of *cassie bush* mark the landsscape and, at times, the road follows along the coastline offering spectacular views of the Atlantic Ocean. Take your time exploring what locals call "the country". Shoot pool in Willikies at Sweet Deals Tavern (pg 114) or enjoy the views from Seatons Village. Half Moon Bay, one of Antigua's finest beaches, is located here along with the impressive natural formation, Devil's Bridge.

ORIENTATION

 DRIVING DIRECTIONS

From St. John's, take Factory Road passing the Antigua and Barbuda Fire Station on your left and the U.S. Peace Corps office on the right. Continue on Factory Road and the new cricket stadium will be on the left, as well as the notable excursion to the village of Parham. Back on the main road, head towards Long Bay passing Betty's Hope.

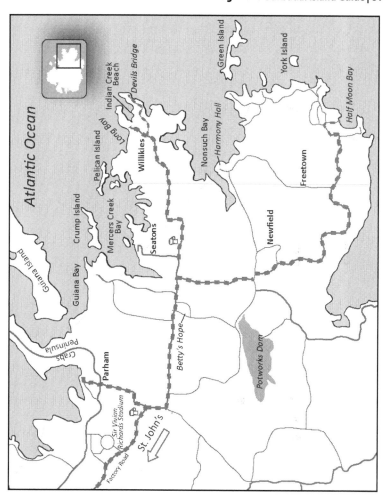

Getting Around

Sample taxi rates (USD, one-way, 4 persons) from St. John's to:
Parham $16
Seatons $19
Devil's Bridge/Long Bay $26
Half Moon Bay/Harmony Hall $28

Bus routes from St. John's (East Bus Station):
#33: Viv Richards Stadium, Betty's Hope, Seatons, Willikies
#31: Potters, Paynters, Parham

Sights

SIR VIVIAN RICHARDS STADIUM

Named after Antigua's most famous cricketer, this impressive stadium was built by the Chinese government for the 2007 Cricket World Cup. It can hold up to 20,000 cricket fans and boasts one of the Caribbean's best party stands with a waterfall, pool and elevated booth for Antigua's favorite DJ, Chickie. Although the state of the art stadium was built for cricket, other sporting events and entertainment are planned for utilizing the facility.

The blue and yellow colored seats angered many ALP supporters who believed the color choice was politically motivated.

PARHAM VILLAGE

DRIVING DIRECTIONS

Taking a left at the fork in the road marked by the bright red *Red Stripe* barbeque stand, the road leads to the village of Parham.

Parham was the earliest commercial settlement on Antigua and local residents claim this village to be Antigua's first capital – historical evidence, however, shows otherwise. Yet with unmarked ruins scattered throughout, Parham feels like it has been around forever. As the island's first port, Parham was the outlet for some 20 sugar estates making it the commercial center on the island at the time. With the decline of sugar and the need for a deep water port, commercial activities were moved to St. John's in the 1920s.

ST. PETER'S CHURCH

When entering Parham, you will notice two large white square columns on your left that mark the entrance to St. Peter's Anglican Church and adjoining cemetery. The famous British architect Thomas Weekes designed St. Peter's after a fire burnt down the original church on this site. St. Peter's Anglican Church stands out with its distinct octagonal shape. The interior holds a beautiful, intricately woven wooden ceiling that has earned this church a stellar reputation across the West Indies. Upon entering the church yard, you will notice the ruins of Parham's first school on your right and the original entrance to the cemetery on your left.

BETTY'S HOPE

From Parham, turn back towards the main road and take a left at the Red Stripe barbeque stand. You will pass through Pares Village before reaching the sign to Betty's Hope on your right.

DRIVING DIRECTIONS

Built in the mid 1600s by Governor Christopher Keynell, Betty's Hope was given to Christopher Codrington in 1674 after the British annulled its land title following a brief French occupation of Antigua. Codrington turned Betty's Hope into Antigua's largest sugar plantation employing at any given time 85% of the population throughout its 270 year reign. The two giant windmills worked in tandem crushing up to 70 cartloads, or two acres, of sugar cane per day.

During the decline in sugar prices and increasing competition of the 1920s, Betty's Hope closed its doors and the sugar estate became neglected. Many of the buildings and materials were eventually used for scrap during the Second World War by U.S. forces stationed on the island.

It wasn't until 1990 that the Betty's Hope Trust formed to undertake the preservation of the estate. Mobilizing government entities, foreign aid, local businesses and volunteers, the Trust was able to partially restore Betty's Hope by 1994 and won the ecotourism award from *Island Magazine* in 1996.

Today, however, many of these preservations are showing signs of age. Trails leading around the estate are overgrown, the informational signs have

TIP Check out the flora around the plantation as they have been labeled with local remedies for common ailments.

faded and can be difficult to read, and forget about using the restrooms. But the visitors center houses many interesting primary documents – including lists of slaves, proclamations and period photographs of the estate – along with a history of slavery, sugar and the plantation itself. The restored sugar mill should also not be missed as it has been well maintained and is the only restored sugar mill on the island.

SEATONS VILLAGE

 DRIVING DIRECTIONS

Continue on the main road and take a left at the charming St. Philip's Church (you will also notice the signs at the junction to Stingray City).

A sign when you are entering this village reads "good times guaranteed here in Seatons". At first glance you might think the person writing that sign had his tongue firmly in his cheek, but this sleepy coastal village's charm is in its slow pace and ease of life. Enjoy some local food and a cold drink at the Sea View Supermarket and Snackette (pg 114) while taking in views over the North Sound Islands. If you are up for an adventure, head down to Stingray City (pg 101) or checkout Paddles (pg 98) for an eco-excursion.

The monkeys and parrots around the ground Stingray City may be the closest thing Antigua has to a zoo.

NORTH SOUND ISLANDS

The North Sound encompasses 15 islands covering 1,000 acres of abundant marine wildlife. The islands are home to a variety of rare species, like the Antiguan Racer snake and the West Indian whistling duck. All of the islands are uninhabited yet tour operators offer trips to several of the protected islands. For organized tours to the islands, see *Eco-Tours* on page 98.

Great Bird Island

Attracting nearly 20,000 visitors to its shores every year, Great Bird Island is the most popular of the

North Sound Islands. Several tour operators offer packages to the 20 acre island that typically include a picnic lunch and snorkeling with ample time to explore the tiny island and its two beaches. In addition to being the only place on earth where the Antiguan Racer snake is found, the island provides sanctuary to several species of lizards, the rare West Indian whistling duck, brown pelicans and frigate birds.

Hell's Gate

You couldn't really call this an island, but the natural 20ft coral archway is an interesting specimen of natural erosion. Calm waters perfect for snorkeling, reside on one side of the archway, while the other side holds the rough and violent Atlantic. Hence, Hell's Gate. It is also said that the water is so deep alongside the formation that the depth reaches Hell. Whatever the reason, you can swim to the rock and relax in a small calm pool under the archway and even climb to the top (careful, the path is narrow and slippery).

Guiana Island

The largest of the North Sound Islands, Guiana Island is home to several on- and off-shore species of wildlife. Small stingrays can be viewed through the crystal clear waters and the sprawling mangroves offer a natural environment for an abundance of marine life. Fallow deer were introduced to the island by the Codrington family and today there is still a wild herd roaming the grounds. There have been several proposals to develop the uninhabited island, but none have materialized to date.

DEVIL'S BRIDGE

From Seatons, head back to the main road and continue through Willikies. After passing the

DRIVING DIRECTIONS

village, keep an eye out on the right for the road leading to Devil's Bridge.

Devil's Bridge formed due to water and wind erosion over hundreds of years, creating a "bridge" between two cliffs. Visitors can actually walk out onto the bridge, but the risk is significant with unpredictable waves crashing against the rocks and a very slippery surface. Devil's Bridge also allows for an impressive vantage point of the rough Atlantic breaking against the barrier reef protecting Antigua.

INSIGHT

Island Legend

Legend has it that African slaves would throw themselves from the bridge into the rough waters in a desperate suicide attempt. Locals would claim that such terrible events could only occur where the devil exists. Today, as the legend goes, if you kneel down, placing your ear to the surface of the bridge, you can hear the moaning of dead African souls.

ISLAND PROTECTORS

In 1964 Cyril "Taffy" Bufton and his wife, Lorna, accepted an offer to manage a small cotton farm for the British owners on Guiana Island. At first the couple from Wales assumed the role of sole caretaker of only the cotton farm, but as the only resident they eventually adopted the entire 460-acre island. The Buftons tamed and fed the fallow deer, protected the West Indian whistling duck, and ensured the vulnerable ecosystem of the island thrived. All while living in a small bungalow with no plumbing and relying on rain for drinking water.

The Buftons lived this way for over 30 years. Then, in 1997, the Antiguan government sought to allow a Malaysian company to develop Guiana Island and 9 other offshore sites into a US$300 million mega resort. The Antiguan Parliament quickly passed a Resettlement Act giving the Buftons a home on Antigua with 5 acres of land plus a monthly income. The Buftons refused to leave claiming squatters rights. One day, beset with anger over the Bird government's attempt to develop his island home, Taffy Bufton walked into the office of Vere Bird Jr, brother of the then Prime Minister Lester Bird, and shot him in the throat. Bird survived and Bufton was arrested for attempted murder. After the incident, the United Progressive Party committed itself to protecting Guiana Island and today the isle remains undeveloped. Bufton was later acquitted and passed-away in 2001.

INDIAN TOWN
The area around Devil's Bridge is Indian Town National Park, established in the 1950s and so named after an archaeological excavation exhumed Arawak artifacts. In 1978 a group of archaeologists from Yale University further excavated the site and discovered several artifacts strengthening the idea that a small community of Arawaks lived here. It is believed that they lived off the abudance of natural resources supplied by surrounding mangroves. When the mangroves eventually silted and Carib attacks increased, the Arawaks were forced to leave the site for survival.

INDIAN CREEK (BEACH)
Protected from the rough Atlantic waters by a natural reef, Indian Creek is hidden down a winding path as you drive towards Devil's Bridge (look for two small boulders on the left). Locals have coined it "Lover's Beach" for its seclusion. The gig is almost up as an expansive hotel is in development for this secret hideaway. The beach will, however, remain public for all to enjoy.

LONG BAY
Long Bay (or Pineapple Beach) is well developed and often crowded. This is mainly due to the all-inclusive Occidental Grand Pineapple Resort, which stretches over nearly half of this large beach, and the Long Bay Hotel on the opposite end. But if you are in the mood for some company, Long Bay has a fun atmosphere with plenty of people playing on the beach or splashing in its calm waters. There are also a couple of good eating and drinking spots (see *Eating* pg 114) along with Island Water Sport Rentals offering snorkeling equipment, kayaks, jet skis and water skiing.

Day Passes

If you plan to stay the whole day at Long Bay, you may want to consider a day pass to the Occidental Grand Pineapple Resort. A day pass goes for about US$50 (plus a 15% sales tax) and gets you all access to all the resorts amenities including non-motorized water sports (not to mention all the food and drinks you can consume). See page 98 for more information on day passes.

HARMONY HALL

Located on the site of an old sugar plantation, Harmony Hall is a restaurant, hotel and art gallery all in one. The stunning views over Nonsuch Bay and adjacent local art gallery, housed in a 1843 plantation house, are worth the drive to its remote location and its Italian cuisine has received rave reviews. You can enjoy a drink on top of its renovated sugar mill and, if you have time, take the ferry service to Green Island for a little exploring and snorkeling.

Protected from the Atlantic Ocean by an expansive reef, Green Island is ideal for snorkeling.

HALF MOON BAY

Arguably Antigua's finest beach, this crescent shaped gem offers some of the island's only body boarding and surfing on its rolling waves. But if you want something a little more relaxing, head south (right when facing the water) until you reach calmer waters buffered by a coral reef. You will also notice the Half Moon Bay Hotel, which was deserted in 1995 after Hurricane Luis destroyed much of it. You can still explore the grounds and even inside the hotel where welcome signs and notice boards remain eerily untouched.

NORTH SIDE

Introduction

The north coast of Antigua lacks the local personality of other areas on the island, but has some interesting spots that are worth a visit. Live music at Miller's By the Sea and the bustling Dickenson Bay offer some great entertainment. You can kite surf at the windy Jabbawock Beach or take a trip out to Jumby Bay to sunbathe with celebrities. The U.S. Air Station is located here along with the tranquil St. Georges Church.

ORIENTATION

From St. John's head north on Popeshead Street passing the infamous Wendy's brothel on your left until the street turns into Fort Road. Take a left at the fork in the road indicating Miller's By the Sea and keep to your left until you reach Fort James Beach. After exploring the area, head north past Runaway Bay and Dickenson Bay before navigating through the northern coast and the hotel-lined Hodges Bay. Cross Airport Road and head towards St. Georges Church resting above Fitches Creek.

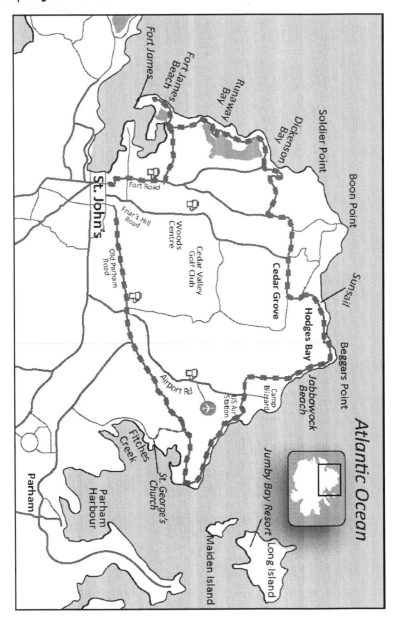

Getting Around

Sample taxi rates (USD, one-way, 4 persons) from St. John's to:

V.C. Bird Int'l Airport $11
Fort James/Dickenson Bay $12
Jabbawock Beach: $15

Bus routes from St. John's (West Bus Station):

Coolidge Bus Company: Wood Centre, V.C Bird Int'l Airport
No bus service to Dickenson and Runaway Bays

Sights

FORT JAMES BEACH

This is the closest beach to St. John's and taxi drivers seem to favor bringing visitors here rather than to more secluded beaches farther away. If this beach was on any other island, it would be pristine. But Antigua's beaches are the best in the world and unfortunately Fort James Beach can't compete with Antigua's elite. It's a nice spot to cool out, but you wouldn't want to spend the day here.

FORT JAMES

With the beach on your right, continue past a row of small, local beach bars until you reach the historic Fort James. Construction of this fort began in 1739 to protect the northern entrance of St. John's Harbour from French pirates who had become accustomed to raiding St. John's. To strengthen the fortification, 17 cannons were erected –

Russell's Bar and Restaurant can be seen from Fort James on a cliff overlooking the bay.

WENDY'S

Just down the street from the Ministry of Social Transformation, where government workers are tackling the island's social injustices, is the island's most recognized brothel, Wendy's. On weekend nights the area around the establishment fills with lingering male figures, and small restaurants have sprouted to cater to this late night crowd. Even though prostitution is illegal on the island, Wendy's has been allowed to continue despite it being a household name.

requiring 11 men to handle each 2-ton cannon – providing such a deterrent that Fort James was never engaged in battle.

Today Fort James is unique as 10 cannons are still on display (guns at other forts were sold as scrap in the late 1800s) and the visitor is able to explore the grounds freely. In fact, a little too freely as Fort James has been in need of a major restoration for several years. A museum is planned for the site to better tell the story of this unique heritage site.

RUNAWAY BAY

Leave Fort James with the beach on your left and veer left at the junction past Miller's by the Sea. You'll pass a large fenced complex, which is the home of Parliamentary Representative Asot Michael.

Runaway Bay is often rough and uninviting. There are several run-down hotels here and the McKinnon's Salt Ponds on your right make you think twice before stopping. Runaway Bay is, however, home to Rush Nightclub with companion sports bar and casino (pg 120), which gets crowded on weekend nights with a young crowd of expatriates and locals.

INSIGHT

Live Music

Miller's By the Sea is a great place to see local and regional musical acts perform live. Situated at the end of Fort James Beach, Miller's is known to cram over 4,000 spectators – most spilling over onto the beach – during its most popular concerts. Call ☎462-9414 to inquire about upcoming shows.

DICKENSON BAY

Dickenson Bay is arguably Antigua's most developed beach and can get extremely busy during high season. The mile long beach is strewed with restaurants, bars and tour operators giving the willing visitor plenty of options throughout the day. The recently erected and impressive Sandals Resort is located here and the Beach Restaurant (pg 115) is a nice dining spot that turns into a popular nightclub after the dinner rush.

CEDAR VALLEY GOLF CLUB
462-0161; WWW.CEDARVALLEYGOLF.AG

Leaving Dickenson Bay, take a left back onto Fort Road. As you drive along, the Cedar Valley Golf Club is to the right, down Friars Hill Road. The par 70, 18 hole championship golf course is open to public with greens fees starting around US$35.

JABBAWOCK BEACH

Turning around on Friars Hill Road, the road ends at a "T". To the left, the road leads towards the exquisite Blue Waters Hotel (pg 129) and back to Dickenson Bay. To the right the main road runs through Cedar Grove Village, the hotel-lined Hodges Bay, and Jabbawock Beach.

Jabbawock Beach is undeveloped and usually empty. The windy and very rough water is not accommodating for the casual swim, but provides an incredible environment for kitesurfing and windsurfing. If you are up for it, Kitesurf Antigua offers lessons and equipment rental. Look for them at Jabbawock's eastern car park or call ☎720-KITE.

Sailing on the North Coast

If you are interested in taking advantage of the high winds along the northern coast, Sunsail Resort (☎462-6263) offers day passes for about US$120 allowing visitors full access to their facilities For the novice sailor, Sunsail includes lessons to get you going. Breakfast and lunch are also included in the rate.

JUMBY BAY RESORT ON LONG ISLAND

Continuing on the main road, you will notice Jumby Bay Resort sprawled across Long Island. The resort is an ultra exclusive getaway that attracts some of the world's rich and famous. Oprah owns a house here and Eli Manning spent a relaxing weekend at the resort after his team's Superbowl win. If the resort is not "full" (code for being closed due to a celebrity figure), visitors can gain access for the day by calling the resort directly at ☎462-6000.

Continue on the main road until you reach a four way intersection. Camp Blizzard, the old U.S. Navy Base that is now the base for Antigua's Defense Force, is to the left and V.C. Bird Int. Airport is to the right, which leads back to St. John's.

U.S. AIR STATION

Straight ahead and on your right is the U.S. Air Station, home to roughly 100 American military contractors. "The Base", as it is called, is part of a series of satellite tracking stations from Florida to Argentina. The complex includes a massive water catchment and purifying system, an American style saloon, and even tennis courts. But due to new security measures, it is nearly impossible to gain access unless you are invited by a resident.

WOODS CENTRE

Continuing down Friars Hill Road, towards St. John's, is the modern strip mall *Woods* located on the left. Inside is the largest supermarket on the island, the first rate *Epicurean,* stocking every imaginable item (much to the relief of many expatriates craving distant, palpable memories). The *Woods Gallery,* a cooperative of local artists, welcomes patrons to enjoy the various pieces of locally produced artwork in their air-conditioned gallery. There is also an office supply store, a few medical offices, a pharmacy, a Radioshack and even a fast-food court.

THE HOSPITALITY TRAINING INSTITUTE

Just pas the U.S. Air Station and on the left, is Antigua's solution to developing a well trained, professional sector of service industry providers.

With tourism clearly on the horizon for Antigua's economy, The Antigua and Barbuda Hospitality Training Institute opened its doors in 2003 with the purpose of preparing Antiguans for the tourism market. The institute focuses on developing culinary skills, equipping tour operators to be "service ambassadors", and teaching the value of customer service. If you want to be a test subject for students, the institute offers inexpensive three-course lunches on select dates. The meals are prepared by aspiring chefs and served by an attentive student wait staff. Call ☎562-4154 for more information.

MAIDEN ISLAND

Do you ever wish you had your own island in the Caribbean? All it takes is the right connections and, well, several million dollars.

Allen Stanford was literally given Maiden Island by the former ALP government as a token of gratitude for all his investment in Antigua. Although uninhabited, the gesture sent shockwaves through the local population as Maiden Island was revered as a holiday picnic getaway, particularly on Easter weekend. Stanford quickly began devising

---

HAWKSBILL TURTLE PROJECT

From June to September Long Island becomes home to roughly 40-50 endangered Hawksbill sea turtles who arrive on the island to lay their eggs. Since 1987, the Jumby Bay Hawksbill Turtle Project has been monitoring and recording the activities of these rare turtles and has received strong support from various organizations across the island.

For more information visit www.jbhawksbillproject.org or contact the Environmental Awareness Group (☎462-6236, or email: eag@candw.ag) to arrange an opportunity to observe these rare creatures.

plans to build a palatial home on Maiden and needed to develop the land for construction. By bringing in required equipment, much of the coral surrounding the island, which had already been damaged by Hurricane Luis, was destroyed. A small guesthouse was built before construction unexpectedly stopped. Stanford then hired an American company to restore the coral reefs with prefabricated materials designed to mimic real coral in hopes of restoring the natural environment. The restoration project is the world's largest fringing breakwater reef system and much to the elation of environmental enthusiasts, there are now plans to develop the island into a small ecological park.

ST. GEORGE'S CHURCH

Passing the Air Station and staying to the right, take a left where indicated (by a sign) for St. George's Church.

St. George's was erected as a small chapel in 1687 and withstood the elements until a series of hurricanes in 1950 destroyed much of the structure. 15 years later, the church was restored only to suffer considerable damage by Hurricane Luis in 1995. Today the church is beautifully reconstructed and rests in a picturesque setting above Fitches Creek Bay.

ACTIVITIES

Beyond the Beach...

Antigua's tourism sector is gaining significant momentum and, in turn, sprouting several local outfits offering land and sea organized activities. We have included some here, but local entrepreneurial minds are constantly creating new experiences to keep Antigua's visitors entertained.

If you are staying at a resort, there will be plenty of options through the hotel. But if you are looking to book independently, here are some suggestions.

ORGANIZED LAND TOURS

Antigua seems small, but can be deceivingly big with a lot to offer. There are several tour operators offering visitors the chance to see the entire island in all-day packages, or dive into just a slice of Antigua. Most will follow an itinerary outlined in the previous chapters of this book, led by professional local guides. A local lunch is typically included.

Scenic Tours Antigua
764-3060
www.scenictoursantigua.com

Estate Safari Tours
463-2061
www.estatesafari.com

Lawrence of Antigua Tours
464-4428
www.lawrenceofantigua.com

Island Safari
480-1225

Service Ambassadors
Most taxi drivers offering around the island tours have been trained as service ambassadors and are very knowledgeable about their island nation.

For cruise ship passengers, the most notable of these tour operators are the swarms of taxi drivers around Heritage Quay pushing minibus tours of the island. For around US$20-30 per person (prices are set by the government), you'll get a drive through the island with a knowledgeable and professional guide. The tours typically include Fig Tree Drive, Nelson's Dockyard and a beach stop. Other tour routes are also available.

ALL-INCLUSIVE DAY PASSES

If you aren't staying at an all-inclusive resort but still want to experience one, even just for a day, there are two well-known resorts offering day passes for non-guests. The passes provide access to all the hotel amenities, including non-motorized water activities, with all meals and drinks included. Each resort offers several different day packages depending on the times you wish to visit. Come early to have breakfast and stay all day, or arrive mid-morning and stay until dusk. Prices will range from US$45-75 per person depending on the season and which package you choose. Call resorts to inquire.

Grand Pineapple Beach Resort (pg 129)
Long Bay; 562-5442
www.grandpineapplebeachresort.com

Jolly Beach Resort (pg 124)
Jolly Beach; 462-0061
www.jollybeachresort.com

ECO-TOURS

Most eco-tour operators focus on exploring the diverse ecosystems around the North Sound Islands without forgetting about the snorkeling and occasional deserted beach. Different packages are available, from half-day tours to full-day excursions with lunch typically included.

Eli's Adventure Antigua
726-6355

www.adventureantigua.com

Eli, a former Antiguan Olympian, started this outfit after spending his entire life on the waters around Antigua. It has since grown it into the island's most popular eco-tour.

Paddles Eco Kayak Tour
463-1944

www.antiguapaddles.com

A one-stop-shop for ecotourism on the island, Paddles offers a half-day tour taking the visitor kayaking, snorkeling and uninhabited island exploring. A snack and rum punch are provided after the excursions.

DEEP SEA FISHING

Antigua's warm clear waters make it an ideal place for visitors looking to land the big one or just enjoy a day out on the open waters. Fish include marlin, tuna, wahoo, shark and barracuda. Most fishing charters include, or will arrange, lunch and drinks. Be sure to inquire what is included in your cost before booking. Here are a couple organized and friendly local charters.

Overdraft Deep Sea Fishing
464-4954
www.antiguafishing.com

Nightwing Charters
464-4665
www.fishantigua.com

CATAMARAN TOURS

Catamaran tours offer an early morning sail that turns into a snorkeling expedition with lunch and finishes with plenty of rum punch onboard the ship into the late afternoon. If you are looking for a lively atmosphere, then these tours are right for you as they are typically crowded. All day cruises cost between US$90-120 per person, depending on the tour option chosen. Rate is all-inclusive, including lunch and drinks

Wadadli Cats
462-4792
www.wadadlicats.com
The most popular of the catamaran tours, Wadadli Cats offers several excursions ranging in cost from US$95-110 per person. The full day sails are typically crowded with all age groups.

Treasure Island Cruises
461-8675
www.treasureislandcruises.ag
Another popular outfit, Treasure Island Cruises costs US$110-140 per person and is usually less crowded than Wadadli Cats (yet offering carbon copy cruises).

Pirates of Antigua
562-7946
www.piratesofantigua.com
Set sail on the 89ft sailing schooner Black Swan (that's right, she isn't a catamaran) for a day of eating and drinks. With a plank and rope swing to entertain bereaved visitors, this 1919 ship has been rigged as a modern day pirate ship. Costs range from the US$60 night cruise to a US$95, five hour day tour.

Night Cruises
Many catamaran tours also offer night cruises on select days. Most will leave from St. John's for a 3-4 hour all-inclusive moonlight cruise. Inquire with companies for more information.

PRIVATE YACHT CHARTERS
There are several privately run yacht charters on the island, mostly on 40ft+ sailboats. Ranging in price from US$75-150 per person, most accommodate up to 10 persons for a private sail the smooth Caribbean Sea and then anchor for snorkeling with lunch and drinks served. If you are looking to get out on the water but avoid the crowded group tours, then private yacht charters offer a great alternative for around the same cost.

Jabberwocky Yacht Charters
764-0595

www.adventurecaribbean.com

Kaye and Nick will take your party out for a day of sailing and snorkeling. They will even cook you up a gourmet lunch. Drinks are included in the price.

Ivy Yacht Charter
464-6327

www.antiguayachtcharter.com

Ivy is a 47-foot sailing yacht, available for full-day, half-day and sunset charters. Inquire about customizing your tour.

Sea Spa Charters
562-5340

www.seaspacharters.net

If you prefer the roar of a powerboat, then Sea Spa Charters will provide you with a day charter to fit your needs. Half and full day charters available. A customized meal is included.

SCUBA DIVING

Antigua is an ideal place to scuba dive with clear, warm waters, an abundance of marine life, and a natural reef surrounding the island. There are also several ship wrecks to explore.

From around US$100 per person, local dive companies offer flexible services from providing equipment rentals for experienced divers to full day courses for the novice.

Jolly Dive
462-8305

www.jollydive.com

Dive Antigua
462-4383

www.diveantigua.com

HIKING

Antigua's natural beauty and relatively flat surface offer a great opportunity to explore the island on foot. Trekking through verdant foliage, resting on hilltop vistas, and discovering hidden beaches are all part of the hiking experience on Antigua. Unfortunately the numerous hiking trails that cut across the island are not well organized nor documented. It is recommended to become well orientated before exploring on your own and to carry plenty of water.

The Historical and Archaeological Society of Antigua
St. John's; 462-1469.

This non-profit organization arranges hiking treks to Antigua's historical landmarks such as British forts and Amerindian sites, along with exploring off-shore islands. The Society can arrange a tour for your group or a visitor may opt to join the Society on a scheduled excursion. A reasonable donation to the organization is required.

Nelson's Dockyard National Park
English Harbour; 460-1379

From Shirley Heights to Pigeon Beach and everything in between, Nelson's Dockyard has several trails for the intrepid hiker. The footpaths stretch from a quarter mile to just under two miles. Check with the park office at the entrance to the Dockyard for more information or call the National Parks Authority directly at ☎460-1379.

Antigua Hash Harriers
www.antiguahash.org

The Antigua chapter of the Hash Harriers – a group developed in Malaysia in the 1930s by expatriates seeking camaraderie – get together every other Saturday for an afternoon hike. The 2-3 hour run/walk concludes with a barbeque. Treks are free of charge, but bring your own eats for the after hike festivities.

OTHER STUFF

Stingray City
Seatons; 562-7297
www.stingraycityantigua.com

If you are up for a little adventure, head down to Stingray City where you can swim with stingrays and snorkel in pristine waters. While you are there, check out their monkeys and parrots, which may be the closest thing Antigua has to a zoo.

Antigua Rainforest Canopy Tour
Fig Tree Drive; 562-6363
www.antiguarainforest.com

Antigua's only zip line canopy tour, this 21 stage thrill ride zips the rider above and through the verdant forest surrounding Fig Tree Drive. The costs vary depending on how much of the course you utilize. Reservations are recommended.

Caribbean Helicopter Ltd.

Jolly Harbour; 460-5900
www.caribbeanhelicopters.net
This helicopter tour company will show you the island from high above. They will also take you over to Montserrat (pg 64) for a closer look at the active volcano, or design a tour just for you.

Spring Hill Riding Club

English Harbour; 460-7787
Headquarters of the Antigua and Barbuda Horse Society, Spring Hill is the most reputable riding club on the island. They will arrange a custom ride, or you can choose from several packages. Since the club is based in English Harbour, there is plenty of options like riding up to Monk's Hill to explore Great George Fort, or making the trek to the deserted Rendezvous Bay. Call in advance to make your reservation.

King's Casino

St. John's near Heritage Quay; 462-1727
It may not be Las Vegas but if you are looking to earn some extra cash quick, King's Casino is the place to go. Located right on the water in St. John's, King's Casino has everything from slot machines to Caribbean stud poker. The casino can get crowded on weekend nights with a sophisticated Antiguan crowd enjoying live music. Although allowed, beach attire and shorts are discouraged.

EATING

Orientation

Eating in Antigua and Barbuda can be extremely satisfying and enjoyable, when guided in the right direction. With world class restaurants serving the best in fine dining and local joints dishing up large portions of a cultural treat, Antigua has delicious cuisine for all budgets.

Price Guide (per person in US Dollars; 1USD = 2.7EC)

$ – under $5
$$ – $5 - 10
$$$ – $10 - 20
$$$$ – $20 and up

ST. JOHN'S

St. John's is loaded with inexpensive local restaurants offering takeaway style meals (seating at local takeaway places is usually available, but limited). If you need help with your selection, just ask your server who is usually more than happy to assist. Like all businesses in St. John's, restaurants are closed on Sunday.

The Home Restaurant ($$$$)

Gambles Terrace; 461-7651
Open Mon-Sat for dinner; reservations required
Located in the boyhood home of Chef Carl Thomas, The Home Restaurant offers an eclectic menu of authentic West Indian dishes including conch salad, Carib gumbo, lobster and other fresh fish. Appetizers start around EC$20 with main courses around EC$50-60. Call first to check availability.

Papa Zouk ($$$)

Gambles Terrace; 464-6044
Open Tue-Sat for dinner 7pm-10pm
You may think you have stumbled into a local rum shop when entering Papa Zouk (*zouk* is French creole music), but this island favorite serves up ultra fresh fish with a creative French creole twist. Try the carnival seafood platter, fresh snapper, or grilled mahi mahi. The extensive rum collection behind the bar puts a nice touch on the décor, but the Ti-punch is the house special.

The Coast ($$-$$$)

Heritage Quay; 562-6278
Open Tue-Sat for lunch and dinner
A popular restaurant with patio seating right on the water. The menu offers a variety of choices including sandwiches, pastas and pizzas. Main courses feature fresh catch and lobster.

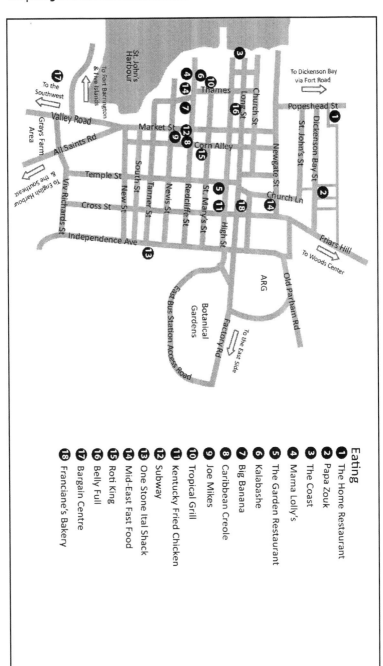

Eating

1. The Home Restaurant
2. Papa Zouk
3. The Coast
4. Mama Lolly's
5. The Garden Restaurant
6. Kalabashe
7. Big Banana
8. Caribbean Creole
9. Joe Mikes
10. Tropical Grill
11. Kentucky Fried Chicken
12. Subway
13. One Stone Ital Shack
14. Mid-East Fast Food
15. Roti King
16. Belly Full
17. Bargain Centre
18. Franciane's Bakery

Mama Lolly's Vegetarian Café ($$)

Inside Redcliffe Quay; 562-1552
Open Mon-Sat for lunch

A vegetarian joint that offers tasty treats for omnivores and vegans alike. The wide selection is ala carte, so walk up to the counter and point to what looks tasty. Or ask the friendly staff for advise.

The Garden Restaurant and Bar ($$)

High St between Temple St and Cross St; 562-2500
Open Mon-Sat for lunch

A great place to try local foods in a comfortable and friendly environment. All the local favorites are available and some have taken on a new twist. Try the mashed breadfruit with salt fish or the fresh catch of the day. Relax outside in the large outdoor seating area with plenty of shade to keep you cool.

Kalabashe ($$)

Vendors Malls on Redcliffe St; 562-6070
Open Mon-Sat for lunch

Taking its name from the Calabashe, an eating utensil of African heritage, this vegan and vegetarian restaurant serves diverse international dishes with an emphasis on Caribbean flavors. Smoothies and shakes are also available from fresh ingredients.

Big Banana Pizzas in Paradise ($$)

Lower Redcliffe St; 480-6985
Open Mon-Sat for lunch and dinner

A local pizza place, Big Banana is a favorite among locals and visitors alike. The restaurant recently relocated to a contemporary building on Redcliffe Street to accommodate the increasing demand of customers. The pizzas come with the standard toppings yet the open-air dining area overlooking busy Heritage Quay makes up for the lack of creativity in the kitchen.

Caribbean Creole Cuisine ($$)

Redcliffe St; 462-5825
Open Mon-Sat for lunch

Tucked away off Redcliffe Street, a visitor could easily miss this hidden gem but the locals find it with ease every time. Large portions of local food include stewed chicken, lamb and steamed fish each served with all the local fixins. Try a cheese filled *bake* and grab a chair on their outdoor patio.

Joe Mikes Restaurant ($$)

Nevis St and Corn Alley; 462-1142
Open Mon-Sat for lunch

This restaurant and casino is a favorite among working locals and can be crowded on weekdays around lunch. You can choose from a selection of local dishes like ducana, mashed fig and the ever popular baked chicken. Seating is available outside on the veranda.

Tropical Grill ($$)

Thames St by Heritage Quay; 562-4252
Open Mon-Sat for lunch

Local lunches that include curried goat, spicy chicken wings and barbeque chicken are offered in take-away containers. Sides include macaroni pie and pasta or potato salads. The affordable price and big portions make this a nice option, but you may be looking for a place to sit as seating on Thames Street is very limited.

Kentucky Fried Chicken - KFC ($$)

Upper High St; 481-1541
Open daily for lunch and dinner

Locals swear it's better down here than up north, and they may be right. The rumor is that the chicken is infused with hot sauce giving it a Caribbean kick. If you're going around lunch or dinner expect long lines as locals love their "Kentucky".

Subway Sandwiches ($$)

Redcliffe St; 562-5539
Open daily for lunch and dinner

This American sandwich chain opened its doors in 2005 and Antiguans have flocked to it since.

Offering the same submarine sandwiches as popular shops up north, you won't be surprised here. But the large air-conditioned dining area is an attractive incentive.

One Stone Ital Shack ($)
Independence Ave and Tanner St; 772-2698
Open Mon-Sat for lunch
Ital has nothing to do with Italian food, but rather has its roots in the Rastafarian community. Serving pastas, beans, salads and "seasoned chunks" out of clay pots and under an outdoor canopy, you can taste some home-cooked Rastafarian food as if Bob Marley was right beside you.

Mid-East Fast Food ($)
Two locations: Redcliffe Quay, 562-3663; Newgate St, 562-0101
Open Mon-Sat for lunch
Don't let the name deceive you. This small establishment offers local take-away lunches from EC$12 that include macaroni pie, small salad, rice and your choice of meats from spicy chicken wings to curried goat. They also have some Middle Eastern dishes including shawarmas, falafels and main courses. Outdoor seating in Redcliffe Quay is available but limited.

Roti King ($)
St. Mary's St and Corn Alley; 462-2328
Open Mon-Sat for lunch
These West Indian burrito look-a-likes are filled with your choice of curried beef, chicken or vegies and wrapped in a warm flour shell. A definite must while in the Caribbean and Roti King serves up the best. A local favorite.

Belly Full ($)
Lower High St
Open Mon-Sat for lunch
Jamaican jerk patties are the only thing on the menu at this fast food restaurant. A few stools line the wall so don't expect a place to sit. But if you want a cheap and tasty pick me up, this is it. Beef, chicken or vegetarian patties are baked in a flaky crust for around EC$5 each. A great treat to

taste while exploring the streets of St. John's. We recommend the veggie patty.

Franciane's Bakery ($)
Two locations: Heritage Quay, 562-5633; Long St at Cross St, 462-2253
Open Mon-Sat for breakfast and lunch
Emulating a French bakery, this sandwich shop and bakery offers made-to-order deli sandwiches on fresh bread and has a nice selection of pastries. Daily lunch specials are also available.

Bargain Centre Supermarket ($)
Behind West Bus Station; 481-4492
Open daily from 8:00am-10:00pm
For the true budget traveler or the curious tourist, this grocery store is the main supermarket for locals. Barbeque chicken, fries, roti, pizza and other ready-to-eat items are available at discount prices. When ordering you may have to fight your turn with local patrons but if you aren't bashful, you should be served quickly. Cold drinks are available at the cheapest prices on the island. After exiting the store, there is a small picnic area upstairs where you can bask in your savings. Shop around the grocery section to check out the chicken feet, pig ear, cow foot and other local ingredients to see what West Indian cooking is all about.

Shawarma
Middle eastern merchants have recently started selling the staple fast food of their home countries, the shawarma, all over St. John's. The specially seasoned meat, typically chicken, is cooked on vertical broilers then rolled with cabbage and a special sauce in a pita. Ask for it hot or mild.

SOUTHWEST
This side of the island offers a lot of choices for the hungry and weary traveler. Colorful beach bars and upscale restaurants share the same stretch of sand. The views at sunset also make this a very attractive spot to enjoy your dinner as the sun dips into the Caribbean Sea.

Sheer Restaurant ($$$$)

Valley Church; 562-2400
Open daily for dinner; reservations recommended
Cut into a sheer cliff, this upscale restaurant is one of Antigua's finest and most ambitious. The menu of Caribbean cuisine with international flavors has won praise from travelers and local residents. The six private, open air pavilions overlooking the Caribbean Sea are just the right touch.

Castaways Beach Bar and Restaurant ($$$)

Jolly Beach; 562-4445
Open daily for lunch and dinner
This isn't the typical beach bar that you will find down the coast. This comfortable spot serves up everything from sandwiches and pizza to steak and seafood feasts. Although it may be a bit more expensive than other beach establishments, the friendly and courteous service coupled with the quality of food make it worth the price.

Turner's Beach Restaurant ($$)

Turner's Beach; 462-9133
Open daily for lunch and dinner
This open air restaurant right on Turner's Beach is an attractive option on a cool, clear night. The menu features conch fritters, fish cakes, fresh fish and grilled lobster. Inquire about their weekly lobster buffet.

OJ's ($$)

Johnson's Point; 460-0184
Open daily for lunch and dinner
The views over the Caribbean Sea and the well decorated, laid back atmosphere almost make up for the overpriced and uncreative menu. The setting is great for a late afternoon drink. If you plan on eating, however, try the snapper.

Darkwood Beach Bar ($$)

Darkwood Beach
Open daily for lunch
Location is everything when it comes to this unpretentious beach bar and restaurant. You won't find a lot of extras, but you'll appreciate

the laid back atmosphere. The bar serves up local drinks with a nice rum punch and the kitchen has a variety of sandwiches and some main courses. It's nothing fancy, but feels right on one of Antigua's most beautiful beaches.

The Epicurean ($)

Jolly Harbour; 462-7705
Open daily 8am-8pm
Looking for a picnic on the beach? Stop by the contemporary Epicurean Supermarket and pick up sandwiches, burgers, fries, barbeque chicken, roti and other prepared eats. You can even buy disposable coolers and ice to keep your drinks cold all day. This is an affordable opportunity to stock up before heading out for a day of beach hopping.

Beach Bars

Almost every beach on the southwest has a beach bar serving inexpensive hamburgers, grilled chicken and sandwiches, with all the local fixings.

SOUTHEAST

English Harbour offers several dining options from high-end upscale restaurants to roadside, takeaway stalls. Many of the restaurants are owned and operated by expatriates who have incorporated European culinary techniques with local Caribbean flavor.

Abracadabra Restaurant ($$$$)

English Harbour; 460 - 2701 (closed June-Nov)
www.theabracadabra.com
Open Mon-Sat for breakfast, lunch and dinner
A popular upscale restaurant with a casual atmosphere, the menu features homemade pastas and fresh fish cooked to perfection. The dining area is separate from the bar, which gets crowded after 10pm. Reservations recommended.

Club Havanna, Mexican Cantina & Bar ($$$)

English Harbour; 725-2308
Open Mon-Sat for lunch and dinner
Specializing in (you guessed it) Mexican cuisine

the menu also spices things up with specials like steak and seafood, including lobster.

Cloggy's ($$$)
English Harbour; 463-8083
Open Mon-Sat for lunch. Breakfast on Sat only
Cloggys serves up fresh ingredients with a European flair. The Dutch owners create tasty sandwiches, salads and other light offerings. There is limited outdoor seating and, as an expatriate favorite, it can get crowded on Saturdays.

Trappas Restaurant & Bar ($$$)
English Harbour; 562-3534
Open daily for dinner
A great place for dinner, the menu offers something for everyone and in adequate portions. The chef has found the perfect fusion between Caribbean cuisine and international influences.

Last Lemming Bar & Restaurant ($$$)
English Harbour; 460-6910
Open daily for lunch and dinner, Sun brunch
The lunch and dinner menus include fresh fish, sushi and mussels. Check out their Sunday brunch beginning at 10:30am.

Bumpkins Beach Bar ($$)
Pigeon Beach; 562-2522
Open daily for lunch and dinner
This restaurant and bar sits at the end of Pigeon Beach. The menu isn't anything to rave about with sandwiches and local dishes, but you can't beat the location.

Grace Before Meals ($)
English Harbour
Open Mon-Sat for lunch
A local place with local prices and friendly service. Rotis and stewed meats with the usual fixings are all available along with fresh juices. Limited indoor seating is available.

Dockside Grocery ($)
Falmouth Harbour
Open Mon-Sat 9:00am-7:00pm, Sun 9:00am-5:00pm
In the back of this small grocery store, hearty deli

sandwiches are made to order with cold drinks available. You can also stock up before heading out for a day of exploring.

Roadside BBQ!

Keep and eye out for roadside bbq stands as the island becomes littered with them on the weekends. These local fast food spots offer great food at very reasonable prices: usually around EC$6-10 for a large portion of barbeque chicken.

EAST SIDE

The eastern side of the island has significantly fewer options for the hungry traveler. Long Bay, however, has a few good spots to grab some tasty food and one of the island's finest restaurants is located here, Harmony Hall.

Harmony Hall ($$$$)
Nonsuch Bay; 460-4120 (closed June-Nov)
Open daily for lunch, call about dinner availability
With its doors first opening in 1987, Harmony Hall has become one of the finest restaurants on Antigua. It has an eclectic menu featuring Italian foods fused with a Caribbean flare, including homemade pasta and fresh fish. Enjoy a glass of wine with spectacular views over Nonsuch Bay.

Mama Pasta ($$)
Long Bay; 773-0527
Open daily for lunch and dinner
With a great view over Long Bay and ample seating in a festive atmosphere, this outdoor restaurant is definitely worth trying. Italian food and local dishes are available.

Barrows Chill Out Bar ($)
Long Bay; 463-6013
Open daily for lunch
Serving sandwiches, chicken'n chips and local lunches this beach restaurant is an affordable option on one of Antigua's most crowded beaches. Try the steamed snapper, it's a local favorite.

Tropical Time Out: Ice Cream Parlor & Deli ($)
Willikies
pen Mon-Sat for lunch
Colorful decoration and local prices make this a nice spot for a quick bite. Sandwiches, hot dogs and ice cream along with cold drinks are available. Limited outdoor seating.

Snackettes
Every village typically has several local snackettes that are like island fast food. Chicken'n chips, fish cakes, local lunches and jerk chicken are usually available at local prices.

NORTH SIDE
Runaway Bay and Dickenson Bay are home to some of Antigua's best live music, fine dining and nightlife. Miller's by the Sea, Russell's, The Beach Restaurant and several other establishments around Dickenson Bay attract both the island's elite and local characters.

Russell's Bar and Seafood Restaurant ($$$$)
Fort James; 462-5479
Mon-Sat 1:00pm-10:00pm, Sun 5:00pm-10:00pm
Nestled between the historic Fort James and the sea, Russell's has a relaxed, upscale atmosphere with open air seating on a cliff overlooking Fort James Bay. The menu features whelks in garlic sauce for an appetizer and fresh catch of the day or lobster as a main course. Check out Sunday nights when Buell and his "strings that sing" take the stage followed by live jazz music with the Harbour Trio.

The Beach Restaurant ($$$)
Dickenson Bay; 480-6940
Open daily for lunch and dinner
Located right on the shores of Dickenson Bay, The Beach lets you eat contemporary entrées while resting your feet in the sand. The food is worth the price and the menu boasts of sushi, pastas, main entrées, sandwiches and pizzas.

Coconut Grove ($$$)

Dickenson Bay; 462-1538
Open daily for breakfast, lunch and dinner
Situated in a tropical setting on Dickenson Bay, this open air restaurant has a casual feel with a strong menu. The lobster thermidor is rumored to be the best in the Caribbean and with other specials like coconut shrimp and beef tenderloin, it's bound to be a hit with everyone.

Sticky Wicket ($$$)

V.C. Bird Int'l Airport; 481-7000
Open daily for lunch and dinner
This unique restaurant sits adjacent to an impressive cricket field and boasts a mouth watering menu that includes a variety of salads, creative sandwiches and generous main courses. Large portions make the prices reasonable and the cricket themed décor is easy on the eyes. A great place for a family lunch.

Miller's By the Sea ($$-$$$)

Runaway Bay; 462-9414
Open daily for lunch and dinner
Along with its reputation as a great place to see live music, Miller's is known as a fine dining spot that is open daily for lunch and dinner. Situated on Fort James beach, Miller's offers a more sophisticated menu than an average beach bar.

Chippy Fish & Chips ($$)

Dickenson Bay Area; 560-2334
Open Mon and Wed 4:00pm-9:00pm
Twice a week David and Jane park their mobile kitchen trailer in a vacant lot near Dickenson Bay and serve up their famous fish'n chips along with other casual eats like lobster bites and kidney pies.

DRINKING & NIGHTLIFE

Orientation

From street vendors selling ice cold beer to beach bars specializing in frozen drinks, Antigua has plenty of spots to grab a Wadadli beer or rum punch. Antigua also has a vibrant nightlife where locals and expatriates converge to drink and dance the Caribbean night away.

ST. JOHN'S

The Coast
Heritage Quay; 562-6278
This restaurant/nightclub has an open air bar that features popular live music on weekend nights. Its trendy, upscale atmosphere attracts the island's best and packs them in until the early morning.

Spliff's Bar and Restaurant
Old Parham Road; 562-5138
Just outside the center of St. John's is a popular local spot featuring live music and weekend barbeques in a comfortable outdoor setting. You won't find many tourists here, making the atmosphere all Antiguan.

Funky Buddha

Lower Redcliffe; 720-0414

Expats tend to flock to this trendy pub in the heart of St. John's. Prices are a little more expensive than a local joint, but a great view from the upstairs deck lets you enjoy a cold drink while watching the traffic below. Open late with daily happy hour. Inquire about karaoke and other themed nights.

C&C Wine Bar

Inside Redcliffe Quay; 460-7025

A surprising treasure for wine lovers tucked away in Redcliffe Quay, C&C offers a variety of wines imported from South Africa with a friendly and helpful staff. Buy a glass or a whole bottle and relax on their outdoor patio.

Ice Cream and More

Thames St in front of Heritage Mall

We enjoy the "more" part with 2for5 Wadadli beers available here. With views of tourists, street vendors and taxi drivers haggling over prices, you can enjoy some of the cheapest beer on the island while stretching out on Thames Street. Just grab your choice of drink from the coolers and take a seat on the open café outside

DOMINICAN BARS

On the southern outskirts of St. John's, on Valley Road, there are a couple of Dominican bars that have ice cold *Presidentes* and a definite Latino feel that contrasts with the cool, laidback Antiguan atmosphere. With built-in speakers and plenty of room to dance, both bars get crowded on weekend nights with a young, lively Dominican crowd.

SOUTHWEST

Dogwatch Tavern

Jolly Harbour; 462-6550

Nestled away among the souvenir shops, is a small drinking spot popular with Jolly Harbour residents. The bar has the usual pub grub along with some entrées. Check them out on Saturday afternoons when the local sailors belly-up after their weekly race.

OJ's
Johnson's Point; 460-0184
The décor and setting of this place is enough for a visit, even if the food doesn't quite come through. With wooden chairs and tables resting on transplanted sand, this restaurant has an upscale beach bar atmosphere. The sea salvage décor is also a nice touch. A great place for a sun downer with superb views over the Caribbean Sea.

Dennis' Cocktail Bar & Restaurant
Ffryes Beach; 462-6740
Antiguan Dennis Thomas moved to this prime spot after running a popular bar in Bolans Villlage. He still offers the same local food and drinks, but now has a view that developers would pay the big bucks to have. It is at least worth a trip to have a drink on the veranda and take in views over Ffryes Bay.

SOUTHEAST

Abracadabra Restaurant & Disco-Bar
English Harbour; 460-2701 (closed June-Nov)
A local favorite with expatriates, "Abras" has a lively outdoor dance floor and themed parties throughout the year. The party starts around 11pm and continues into the early morning hours. If you're in the mood for some nightlife, it is definitely worth the trip. Saturday nights are the most popular.

Club Havanna, Mexican Cantina & Bar
English Harbour; 725-2308
Great atmosphere and EC$5 tequila shots make this a nice stop while you are in English Harbour. You can dance the night away on Wednesday with local bands and enjoy some Karaoke on Thursday nights.

The Mad Mongoose
English Harbour; 463-7900
Known for its happy hour, this spot is a great place to grab a drink. The full menu offers pub grub in good portions and the free Wi-Fi attracts weary sailors trying to connect home.

EAST SIDE

Smiling Harry's Beach Bar
Half Moon Bay

They don't call him Smiling Harry for nothing and his congenial disposition is contagious. Located just up the road from Half Moon Bay, this beach bar has hamburgers until they are "finished". But Harry will serve you up a cold one for the local price and entertain you with stories for as long as you like.

Sea View Supermarket and Snackette
Seatons Village

This local supermarket with adjoining snackette is a nice spot to have a drink while taking advantage of the great views over the North Sound Islands. A few benches are available outside. If you come hungry, you may be disappointed as the snackette only operates on weekends.

Sweet Deal Tavern
Willikies

Locals like to shoot pool and eat at this roadside tavern, which can get a little loud at times with music blaring from speakers overhead. The proprietor will, however, settle things down to make visitors feel comfortable. Good place for the traveler to grab a Wadadli and shoot a game of pool.

NORTH SIDE

The Beach
Dickenson Bay; 480-6940

When the sun goes down, this restaurant by day turns into a hopping dance club at night; it's a favorite of local expatriates. Friday nights are usually crowded with dancing until the morning.

Rush Nightclub
Runaway Bay; 562-7874

Open Thursday through Saturday with local and international DJs keeping the place packed with a young crowd. If you plan to go, leave your beach clothes at home since a dress code is enforced:

no sneakers and no shorts, caps, or vests for men. Cover charge on weekend nights.

Putters

Dickenson Bay Area; 463-4653

Putters is home to Antigua's only mini golf course (EC$15 for a round) and expatriates love it. Happy hour is everyday from 6-7 with EC$5 local drinks and a popular local DJ plays every Wednesday. A full menu is available with entrées, sandwiches and appetizers.

ACCOMMODATIONS

Orientation

Antigua considers itself an "up-market" destination and accommodations are priced as such. It is rare to find anything for less than US$200 a night, even in the low season. Most of the lower-end accommodations are locally owned and operated. If you choose to go this route, we have included several budget spots. But if you want to look out your window and enjoy those picturesque Caribbean views while being pampered by a friendly and courteous staff, then Antigua has got what you need (just be prepared to pay the price).

Price Guide (per night in US Dollars; 1USD = 2.7EC)

$ – $40 - 75
$$ –$75 - 150
$$$ –$150 - 300
$$$$ –$300 – 600
$$$$$ – $600 and up (we aren't kidding!)

REALTY AGENCIES

There are a few realty companies that provide services to visitors interested in renting a private villa, home or apartment. Prices start around US$75 a night (with really no upper limit) with short- and long-term options available.

Island Rentals
463-2662
www.antiguarent.com

English Harbour Realty
562-5333
www.englishharbourrealty.com

Antigua Villa Rentals
464-1510
www.antigua-villa-rentals.com

ST. JOHN'S

St. John's is not the place you would want to spend the night. Restaurants and shops close around 6:00pm on weekdays rendering St. John's a sort of ghost town after dusk. Besides, there isn't a beach within miles and the hotel rates in town are often higher than resorts. But if you find yourself in the capital and need a place to stay, here are a few options.

Heritage Quay Hotel ($$$)
Heritage Quay; 462-1247
www.heritagehotelantigua.com
The hotel of choice for many regional business travelers, Heritage Quay Hotel has modest rooms with air conditioning and kitchenette. The rooms are nothing special but the location overlooking the cruise ship docks can make up for it.

City View Hotel ($$$)
Upper Newgate St; 562-1211
www.cityviewhotelantigua.com
City View, as its name suggests, does offer some pretty amazing views over St. John's. And with a full breakfast included in the rate, you may be pleasantly surprised.

Hibiscus Cottages ($$)
Friars Hill; 560-3534
www.hibiscuscottages.com
These small units are a nice alternative to the

overpriced hotels of St. John's. Each sun-filled studio apartment has full furnishings including a kitchen and air conditioning. Located in a middle-class neighborhood north of St. John's, the nearest beach is a five minute drive away.

SOUTHWEST

The southwest's biggest draw is the amazing sunsets over the Caribbean Sea. The price range for accommodations here can reach exorbitant proportions and may be a turn off for many. There are, however, a few budget alternatives around the Johnson's Point area that are just steps away from the beach. No matter where you choose to stay, the southwest offers a true Caribbean experience.

Hermitage Bay Hotel ($$$$$)
Hermitage Bay; 562 5500
www.hermitagebay.com
Arguably one of the finest and most elite all-inclusive resorts in the Caribbean, these private cottages are nestled in a hillside overlooking the secluded Hermitage Bay.

Carlisle Bay Hotel($$$$$)
Old Road; 484-0000
www.carlisle-bay.com
Once described as the best of the best on Antigua, Carlisle Bay attracts the world's elite and rightly so. Offering a more contemporary European feel than other resorts on the island, Carlisle Bay has become known for its impeccable service and amenities.

Curtain Bluff ($$$$)
Old Road; 462-8400
www.curtainbluff.com
Curtain Bluff is an all-inclusive luxury hotel set on its own bluff overlooking Morris Bay. With a more Caribbean feel than its infamous neighbor, Carlisle Bay, Curtain Bluff offers a great family getaway spot.

Cocobay Resort ($$$$)

Valley Church area; 562-2400

www.cocobayresort.com

With 42 brightly colored, colonial style cabins, each with private patio overlooking Valley Church Beach, this getaway is advertised as the most romantic resort in Antigua. We're not sure about that, but this all-inclusive estate is unique and definitely a destination point.

Cocos Hotel ($$$$)

Jolly Beach; 462-9700

www.cocoshotel.com

Resting on a hilltop, with a beach on each side, these 23 open-air cabins are naturally nestled in a tropical garden and offer spectacular views with a million dollar vantage point for the setting sun. Rate is all-inclusive.

HBK Villa Rentals ($$$)

Jolly Harbour; 462-6166

www.hbkvillas.com

Jolly Harbour's main property management office rents the carbon copy villas that are found throughout Jolly Harbour. You can choose between a standard or luxury villa, each has two bedrooms and two baths with kitchen, all fully furnished (the luxury line includes higher-end furnishings). If you want to be close to the beach, make sure to request a villa in the "south finger".

Jolly Beach Resort ($$$)

Jolly Beach; 462-0061

www.jollybeachresort.com

An all-inclusive resort with a surprisingly better dining experience than the typical all-inclusive Caribbean getaway. The rooms are small, but comfortable and the beach is right at your doorstep. Activities organized daily.

Stoney Hill Studio Apartments ($$)

Caddes Bay area; 562-6500

www.stoneyhillstudioapartments.com

Nestled in the hills in the southwest with a great vantage point to enjoy the sunset, these small self-contained studio apartments are comfortably furnished with a spacious gallery to enjoy your view.

Antigua Budget Rooms ($)

Jolly Harbour; 788-3371

Simple, basic and clean. These rooms and cottages offer budget accommodations within walking distance to Jolly Harbour.

Inn La Galleria ($)

Deep Bay area; 460-6060

www.innlagalleria.com

Small hotel with simple rooms in the hills overlooking deep bay. Each has a/c and some offer spectacular views over the Sea.

3-Martini Apartments ($)

Johnson's Point area; 460-9306

Six large rooms, with balconies overlooking the ocean, offer nice views for the rate. Turner's Beach is a good walk away through the bright and lively Johnson's Point Village and the 3-Martini Bar is right below.

SOUTHEAST

The southeast is a good choice for those who want to be close to the bustling English Harbour and its nightlife. You can also find most of the island's budget accommodations here since the area caters to sailors looking for inexpensive short-term housing before pulling anchor. The one drawback to staying here is the lack of long stretches of white sand beaches that bless the rest of the island.

Inn at English Harbour ($$$$$)

English Harbour; 460-1014

www.theinn.ag

This seemingly small 28 room hotel feels like it was taken right out of Nelson's heyday with all the colonial grandeur. There are the usual amenities and extras for a hotel in this price range, but the old-time charm is what makes this place unique. Set on its own small private beach inside the Dockyard.

Antigua Yacht Club Marina Resort ($$$)

English Harbour; 562-3030

www.aycmarina.com

This sprawling complex offers rooms and suites with views over Falmouth Harbour and within a short walk to the Dockyard. The closest beach is Pigeon Beach, a 10 minute walk away. Rooms are upscale with sleek, modern furnishings.

Oceanic View Vacation Cottages ($$)

Freeman's Village; 562 - 6500

www.oceanicviewantigua.com

Simple 2 and 3 bedroom gingerbread houses in a garden setting. Located near the middle of the island, the closest beach is a drive away. Each cottage contains a full kitchen.

Waterfront Hostel ($)

English Harbour; 460-6575

www.caribbean-hostels.com

Budget accommodations in an ideal location. Rates are US$40/single, US$60/double with private shower in the room but shared toilets. Rooms are simple and clean, with free wireless internet included.

Zanzibar Hotel ($)

Falmouth Harbour; 463-7838

www.zanzibarantigua.com

Budget rooms are available in a large 6-room house, set in a nice garden in Falmouth Harbour. Rooms, starting at US$60 in high season, are nicely furnished, clean and air conditioned. Two private cottages are also available from US$100-200 a night. Wi-Fi available free of charge.

The Anchorage Rooms ($)

Falmouth Harbour; 561-0845

www.theanchroagecentre.com

Located upstairs of a small business complex, these clean and contemporary rooms offer an inexpensive alternative for the budget traveler and their location between both Falmouth and English Harbours provides easy access to all the area has to offer.

EAST SIDE

Accommodations here are focused around Long Bay, the most developed area on this part of the island. If you are looking for an inexpensive option and aren't concerned about being right on the beach, then there are a couple other locally operated spots.

Long Bay Hotel ($$$$)

Long Bay; 463-2005

www.longbayhotel.com

Family owned and operated since 1966, this small hotel has 20 rooms and five cottages situated on a peninsula so all the rooms face the water.

Dian Bay Resort and Spa ($$$$)

Long Bay; 460-6646

www.dianbayantigua.com

This all-inclusive resort and spa has got about everything a visitor could want. If you are looking for a relaxing resort that pampers its guests, then this is a good bet.

Grand Pineapple Beach Resort ($$$$)

Long Bay; 562-5442

www.grandpineapplebeachresort.com

More expensive than its competitors, Grand Pineapple is an all-inclusive resort catering to a more mature clientele looking for a quiet Caribbean getaway.

Ellen Bay Cottages ($$)

Seatons Village; 561-2003

www.ellenbaycottages.com

These three fully furnished two-bedroom units with kitchen are located just off calm waters in Seatons (down "the hill", near Stingray City). Although they are situated right on the water, the closest swimming beach is Long Bay, about 5 minutes away by car.

Willowby Heights Guest Rooms ($$)

Willowby Bay; 560-9738

www.willowbyheights.com

These clean and modest apartments offer some great panoramic views over the Atlantic Ocean. The beach is about a ten minute drive away and the remote location could be a turn-off for some.

NORTH SIDE

Accommodations on this part of the island are focused around the Dickenson Bay area, and rightly so. Restaurants, nightlife and one of Antigua's busiest beaches are all easily accessible here.

Blue Waters ($$$$)

Soldier's Bay; 462-0290

www.bluewaters.net

A hidden luxury getaway on Antigua's north side, Blue Waters has an intimate feel with all the extras. The beach is completely isolated so although it is public, like all beaches on Antigua, it is only accessible to guests. Rate is all-inclusive.

Siboney Beach Club ($$$)

Dickenson Bay; 462-0806

www.siboneybeachclub.com

Located right on Dickenson Bay in a tropical garden setting, this is a great little hotel for couples or anyone wanting a relaxing vacation. A nice alternative to the larger resorts down the beach.

Dickenson Bay Cottages ($$$)

Dickenson Bay; 462-4940

www.dickensonbaycottages.com

This quiet hotel, removed from busy Dickenson Bay, has one and two bedroom units with all the modern amenities including air conditioning. Although the bright floral decorations seem outdated, the clean and relaxing atmosphere makes up for it.

Antigua Village ($$$)

Dickenson Bay; 462- 2930

www.antiguavillage.net

Sitting on the western end of Dickenson Bay, this hotel offers apartment type accommodations (including a small kitchen) on some of Antigua's most valuable real estate.

Galley Bay Cottages ($$)

Galley Bay Beach; 464-6499

Four sea-view cottages are available all completely furnished with dine-in kitchen. Some of the unique furnishings were provided by local artisans giving these cottages a true Caribbean feel.

BARBUDA

Introduction

Barbuda lies just 27 miles to the north of Antigua and is one of the few commercially undeveloped places left in the Caribbean. Miles of unspoiled, "pink" sand beach have made the island famous (crushed pink shells that glisten in the sun make the sand appear pink). There are about 1,500 Barbudans living in the island's capital, Codrington. The rest of the 62 square mile island remains unpopulated, rendering it a quiet, seemingly deserted island in the Caribbean.

Barbuda is relatively flat – the highest point is just 125ft – with low bush covering much of the island. The Highland Area, in the central part of the island, contains fallow deer and wild boar that roam freely, yet are hunted legally. There is limited agriculture on Barbuda making it dependent on Antigua for basic provisions. Fishing, however, is Barbuda's main economic activity with lobster bountiful in the Codrington Lagoon and a variety of sea life off the island's shores.

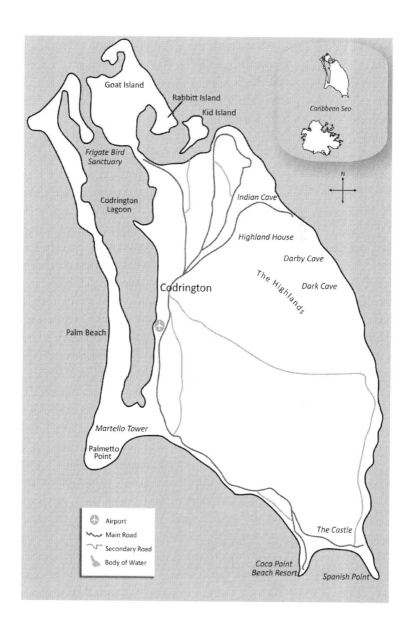

Goat Island

Rabbitt Island

Kid Island

Caribbean Sea

Frigate Bird
Sanctuary

Codrington
Lagoon

Indian Cave

Highland House

Darby Cave

The Highlands

Dark Cave

Codrington

Palm Beach

N

Martello Tower

Palmetto
Point

The Castle

Coca Point
Beach Resort

Spanish Point

⊕ Airport

〰 Main Road

〰 Secondary Road

▨ Body of Water

History

Barbuda's modern history begins with the wealthy Christopher Codrington who established sugar plantations across the Leeward Islands, including Antigua and Barbuda. Barbuda's unfertile soil, however, was not suited for King Sugar, so Codrington set out to make the island a resource for provisioning Antigua. The Africans Codrington brought to the island became herders, hunters and fisherman, while the enslaved Africans on Antigua produced sugar. Some evidence suggests that Codrington, wanting to make the most of his estate, devised a plan to make Barbuda a breeding ground for exporting slaves to other islands. From 1779 to 1834, over 170 Barbudan slaves were sold to plantations across the Caribbean and even to the southern United States.

Codrington's influence on Barbuda is still evident today as the capital takes his name, and his Highland House estate can be explored on Barbuda's highest point.

In 1870, after a 185 year reign, the Codrington family's lease on Barbuda expired yet. The ties between the two islands – due to Codrington's association with each – would lay the foundation for Antigua and Barbuda to become one nation in 1981.

POLITICS

Barbuda has representation in both houses of the Antigua and Barbuda government: the Parliament and Senate. The small island's main governing body, however, is the Barbuda Council. Consisting of 11 members, the Council was established in 1976 by the Barbuda Local Governance Act giving Barbuda extraordinary local authority not enjoyed by the communities of Antigua. The Council regulates all commercial development on the island, along with basic government services like health and infrastructure, and has the power to levy taxes.

Getting There

There are a couple of options for getting to Barbuda, either by boat or air. If you are going just for the day, then flying to the island will save you several hours of time. Carib Aviation offers two daily roundtrip flights to Barbuda from V.C. Bird Int'l Airport. Flights depart Antigua at 8:00am and 6:00pm with returns at 8:30am and 6:30pm from Barbuda. The 15 minute flight costs about US$75/return.

Carib Aviation
V.C. Bird International Airport; 481-2103
www.carib-aviation.com

The Barbuda Express provides roundtrip boat service to the island twice daily for around US$50/return. The 90 minute ride departs Antigua early in the morning and returns around 5pm. The company also offers organized day tours for around US$125 per person (ferry service, tour and lunch included).

Barbuda Express
St. John's; 560-7989
www.antiguaferries.com

Getting Around

If you are planning on exploring the island on your own, the best form of transportation would be car rental for about US$50 a day. You won't find any of the big car rental companies operating on the island, only locally owned and operated set-ups.

BA Tours and Car Hire
Codrington; 783-7243 or 460-0065

There are also several taxi operators offering fixed price tours taking the visitor to Barbuda's attractions, including its deserted beaches. This can be a good way to see the island with a local who knows those hidden spots. A local lunch of fallow deer or even lobster is usually included in the price, but it is good to check in advance. Barbuda's tour operators are jacks-of-all-trades when it comes to entertaining guests and will arrange anything from scuba diving to fishing excursions upon request. Contact them directly for details.

BA Tours and Car Hire
Codrington; 783-7243 or 460-0065

Crystal Bay Tours
Codrington; 724-7490

George Burtons Tours
Codrington; 772-1209

Scuba Diving

With over 300 shipwrecks amongst its reefs, Barbuda is a paradise for scuba divers. If you are a novice, get the experience you need before arriving on Barbuda as certification is not available.

Sights

CODRINGTON VILLAGE

There is not much to see or do in the island's capital, which seems to be almost void of life at times. Locals tend to lime at the pier or have a quiet lunch at The Palm Tree Restaurant (see *Eating*). Your best bet is not to waste time exploring the village, but rather orientate yourself with the island and arrange transportation to go exploring.

FRIGATE BIRD SANCTUARY

Barbuda is home to the largest colony of frigate birds *(Fregata magnificens)* in the world, with an estimated 2,500 birds nesting in the mangroves of Codrington Lagoon. Barbudans have recognized the importance of the natural sanctuary as a tourist attraction and local guides can be hired to take the visitor via boat through the lagoon to the sanctuary.

The aerial acrobatics of the birds, who have the ability to stay in the air for days at a time, rivals any air show in the world. The most impressive time to see the birds is during the mating season (Sept-Jan), when males vie for the affection of the females.

MARTELLO TOWER

Three miles south of Codrington stands a 56ft high Martello tower erected by the British as a defensive lookout point along Barbuda's southern coast. The term "Martello" is derived from the tower at Cape Mortella in Corsica that the British, in 1792, fought to overtake. Impressed with the design of the fortification, the British erected replicas across their colonies and even on the southern coast of England to defend against Napoleon's invasion in 1803.

Although the tower was never engaged in battle, it served as an ideal vantage point for spotting shipwrecks off the coast of Barbuda. Upon sighting a distressed vessel, a signal would be transmitted to the capital. According to the lease agreement Codrington had with the Crown, he was entitled to all shipwrecks off Barbuda's shores.

SPANISH POINT

Spanish Point projects to the most southeasterly point on Barbuda where the Caribbean Sea and

Atlantic Ocean meet. The small peninsula takes its name from the shipwreck of the Spanish ship *Santiago de Cullerin,* which sank in 1685. The ship was rumored to be carrying 13,000 pesos for the Spanish garrisons at Maracaibo; the cargo has never been recovered.

K-Club

In route to Spanish Point, you will pass the infamous K-Club where Princess Diana vacationed. The ultra-opulent resort recently closed, but was considered one of the finest resorts in the world during its peak.

THE CASTLE

Old maps of Barbuda show a formative structure, known as the Castle, constructed of watchtowers and high stonewalls with a courtyard and overseers house. It was here, in 1745, that the island's manager was killed by enraged slaves after it was discovered he had been mutilating and torturing imprisoned slaves. A rebellion ensued and slaves overtook the fortification, occupying the residence and its arsenal of weapons. Soldiers from Antigua were sent and successfully put down the small rebellion. It is said that two slaves, who were identified as masterminding the rebellion, were burned alive at the main gates.

In 1843 an earthquake severely damaged this fortification, bringing down the watchtowers and walls. Today the ruins, although overgrown, can be explored freely.

CAVES

Due to its limestone composite, Barbuda has numerous caves to explore. When exploring the caves, it is recommended to bring a local guide with you for safety and to fully experience natural beauty of these natural occurrences. Some caves, like Darby's Cave, can be inaccessible by car and must be reached on foot.

Darby's Cave

This couldn't really be considered a "cave" but rather a horizontal sinkhole measuring 70ft high and 300ft in diameter. The unique formation offers a tropical, lush interior environment with interlacing trees and foliage.

Dark Cave

Lying just south of Darby's Cave, is a shallow cavern consisting of small pools of water with abundant and rare sea life. Dark Cave can be accessed by crawling through a small opening that leads to an open cavern. Amerindian artifacts, dating back to 800AD, have been discovered nearby making it likely that the early people of this island used the cave as a fresh water source. Today the cave is home to the rare blind shrimps *(Typhlatya monae)* that reside in the cavern's pools. This rare species is known to exist only here and on Mona Island, off Hispaniola.

Indian Cave

Located on the northeast coast, on the other side of the island than Darby's and Dark Caves, Indian Cave has several chambers to explore including the Bat Chamber where bats can be seen hanging from the 35ft high ceiling. But the real draw to the cave are the two petroglyphs inscribed on the caves walls by its first residents, the Amerindians. These rock carvings were intended to protect the

AMERINDIAN ARTIFACT OR DOOR STOP?

A valuable Amerindian stone "Dog's Head" artifact that would have been used by Shamans as a ceremonial inhaler was found near Indian Cave by a local Barbudan who used the piece as a doorstop in his home until it was identified by a visiting archeologist. It is considered to be the only artifact of its kind south of Puerto Rico, and the first evidence of Amerindians living on Barbuda. The piece is now in an exhibition in the United States.

cave from evil spirits and are the only known petroglyphs on Antigua and Barbuda.

HILLHOUSE
Sitting atop the highest point on Barbuda, at 125ft, Hillhouse was built by William Codrington in 1720 as the wealthy family's estate on the island. Remains of the estate can be explored but are overgrown with bush. The highlight of the Hillhouse is the view over the island, which is worth the trip.

Eating and Drinking

Outside of Coco Point Lodge, all eateries are local joints featuring fresh seafood and local meats, in addition to sandwiches and burgers. A hearty portion of rice & beans is included with a small salad or steamed vegetables.

Palm Tree Restaurant ($$)
Codrington; 784-4331
At one time the island's premier local restaurant, to the surprise of many visitors who gawked at the small establishment, the Palm Tree Restaurant serves eclectic local lunches and dinners that feature lobster, turtle and fallow deer.

Wa O'moni ($$)
Codrington; 562-1933
Wa O'moni, the Arawak name for Barbuda, serves an extensive menu of local Barbudan dishes including lobster and conch. Sandwiches and burgers also available.

Green Door Tavern ($)
Codrington; 460-0065
Local tavern in the center of Codrington open seven days a week from 7am till late in the evening. Local meals available with a pool table attracting a popular local crowd.

Accommodations

If you are planning to stay the night or even your entire vacation on Barbuda, the current accommodation situation is not on your side. Recently, Barbuda saw 3 of the island's major resorts close, leaving Coco Point as the only large, commercial set-up left on the island. In response, several enterprising Barbudans have established guest houses in Codrington and even cottages on deserted stretches of pink-sand beach.

Coco Point Lodge ($$$$$)

Coco Point; 462-3816

www.cocopoint.com

Secluded on its own 164-acre peninsula, Coco Point is an all-inclusive resort offering single rooms, suites and multi-bedroom cottages. All of the 34 units are right on the beach and the resort provides a plethora of activities to keep its guests entertained. Guests are met at Codrington Airport before being flown to the resort's private airstrip.

North Beach Cottages ($$$$)

North Beach; 726-6355

info@antiguaadventures.com

If you are looking for seclusion, or perhaps are curious to what it is to be marooned, then you've found it at North Beach Cottages. For about US$400/night, you can rent one of three small cottages set on 23 acres of pristine coast; there is nothing within miles. The cottages are simple and share a common pavilion where the proprietor, a local named Reuben, serves meals and drinks. The rate is all-inclusive.

Palm Tree Guest House ($)

Codrington; 784-4331

Located just outside Codrington, 8 en-suite double rooms are available. Each have a private bath, television, a small kitchen and air conditioning.

Island Guest House ($)

Codrington; 460-0498

Three self-contained rooms with private baths are available above a small business complex in Codrington.

Giving Back: Organizations Making a Difference

Behind those postcard print sunsets and lavish resorts there is another side of Antigua, one that is all too evident for local residents. Antigua is a developing country and while the tourism industry paints a pretty picture of the island, there are significant issues permeating through the country. Poverty, unemployment, illiteracy and crime have had serious implications on the local population. Government ministries, such as Social Transformation and Youth, have attempted to address these issues but lack the resources for widespread treatment. There are, however, several non-governmental organizations (NGOs) working on the grassroots level that are making a difference in the communities they serve. Local organizations rely heavily on private donations to achieve their objectives; the government helps when possible but cannot adequately support NGO initiatives.

Amazing Grace Foundation
All Saint's Road
Belmont; 560-1989
www.amazinggracefoundation.org
Amazing Grace is based in a small, traditional West Indian house which is home to children of special needs. Run by a board of directors (all of whom are volunteers), Amazing Grace fills a public void when it comes to assisting disabled children.

Project Hope Community Resource Centre
Cassada Gardens; 561-3999
www.projecthopeantigua.org
Project Hope is an ambitious public-private partnership between the Government of Antigua and Eric Clapton's drug rehabilitation clinic, Crossroads (which is located on Antigua). The Project Hope Centre provides training, education, awareness and community outreach for the community it serves, Cassada Gardens. There are plans to begin opening several other Project Hopes in vulnerable communities.

Antigua and Barbuda Humane Society

Bethesda; 460-8843

www.antiguaanimals.org

Local treatment and attitude towards dogs coupled with a large stray population makes Antigua a dog lover's nightmare. Not just limiting its services to dogs but to all domesticated animals, The Antigua and Barbuda Humane Society struggles to save as many animals as possible. You will notice donation boxes at the airport and at expatriate establishments (like inside Jolly Harbour's *Epicurean*).

Gilbert Agricultural Rural Development Center (GARD)

Mercers Creek; 463.4121

www.gardc.org

At one time agriculture thrived on Antigua but since the 1980s this vital sector has declined. GARD provides training in practical agricultural techniques and promotes farming as a viable occupation. The Center also assists budding entrepreneurs in selling and marketing their agrobusiness ideas.

Environmental Awareness Group

St. John's; 462-6236

www.eag.org.ag

Home to several rare species, a vulnerable environment and an industry that depends on the state of that environment, the Environmental Awareness Group has its work cut out. To fulfill its mission of conserving the environment of Antigua and Barbuda, the EAG implements a three-pronged approach that includes education, advocacy and environmental protection programs.

About the Author

Christopher Beale

After graduating college and landing an unfulfilling desk job, Christopher set off for the Peace Corps in hopes of an adventure. He would spend the next two years living and working on Antigua and Barbuda while exploring everything the island has to offer. After his service, he continued to live on Antigua where he began to research and write this book. He now lives and writes in Washington, DC, yet continues to travel back to the Caribbean.

Visit us at

www.otherplacespublishing.com

14030722R00087

Made in the USA
Lexington, KY
04 March 2012